# Read for Freedom: A Literacy Model to Reduce the Next Generation of Prisoners

by

Denise Mayo Moore, Ph.D.

# Table of Contents

# List of Tables

# List of Figures

# Abstract

School districts are accountable for students achieving grade-level literacy standards. However, many third-grade students in Sun Valley Lake, New Jersey, are not achieving the No Child Left Behind (NCLB) literacy standard of proficient, which is defined as reading on grade level.

The purpose of this quantitative study was to investigate whether the Success Program was effective at engaging struggling third-grade, African-American students in a supplemental literacy program that can be replicated by school districts with similar demographics. The Success Program's theoretical underpinnings are grounded in Vygotsky's socio-cultural theory and Zone of Proximal Development.

These theoretical frameworks are supported by the Response to Intervention (RTI) model, on which the Success Program is modeled. The conceptual framework in this study is the Resilience model. The students were selected using a nonprobability criterion sampling, which dictates a quasi-experimental design using a pre- and post-test method.

There were 100 students during two consecutive school years; 2010-2011 and 2011-2012. The study results indicated that for each school year, the 50 students who participated in the Success

Program achieved statistically significant higher scores than the 50 students who did not participate for all four study variables: reading comprehension, oral reading fluency, instructional reading level, and sight-word recognition. The quantitative data indicated the Success Program is a viable intervention.

Therefore, this study leads to positive social change by providing educators in Sun Valley Lake as well as the additional 30 Abbott, New Jersey school districts as well as districts nationally with similar characteristics, strategies to increase the literacy skills of third-grade, African-American students.

## Dedication and Acknowledgments

I dedicate this book to my children.

"If you believe, you will achieve."

Dr. Charles Gray has been instrumental since my first semester of undergraduate school. Dr. Gray you have been my mentor for 20 years. You have continually guided me to be a reflective, compassionate practitioner.

Denise Mayo Moore, Ph.D.

## Chapter 1: Introduction to the Study

Educational inequality in the United States has been well documented. In *Brown v. Board of Education* (1954), the U.S. Supreme Court ruled there was inequality in education due to segregation and inferior resources in schools that African-American students attended compared to the schools European-American (Caucasian) students attended. In *Abbott v. Burke* (1981), the State Supreme Court of New Jersey ruled inequality in education existed in 31 school districts. The Abbott decision required the implementation of measures with appropriate funding in the 31 districts recognized by the court and deemed to have special needs (Gomez, 2008). These districts, which could not afford to offer students an adequate education, were considered the poorest in the state (New Jersey), with large minority populations (Gewertz, 2005). The State Supreme Court of New Jersey found there was less funding expenditure per pupil in these special-needs districts than in affluent suburban districts in New Jersey. The New Jersey Department of Education (NJDOE) was ordered to offer all students an equal education by providing a balance of funding and services for supplementing early literacy, health, and social services to these impoverished districts (Gewertz, 2005). The Success Program in the Sun Lake Valley school district, one of the 31 Abbott districts, addressed early literacy deficits in third-grade African-American students.

Many strategies and interventions have been enacted to standardize curriculum ensuring that all students receive an equitable education. The No Child Left Behind Act (NCLB; 2002) was signed into law to ensure children met educational standards in the United States. The No Child Left Behind act mandated school districts to achieve adequate yearly progress (AYP), which meant schools must produce annual incremental improvement in statewide test scores (U.S. Department of Education, 2011). The No Child Left Behind act expected 95% of students to have scored 'proficient or above' in statewide reading, math, and science tests by 2014. A re-authorization

of the Individuals with Disabilities Education
Improvement Act (DEIA) suggested school districts
should use a scientifically-based methodology such
as Response to Interventions (RTI) for implementing
strategies for behavior and learning difficulties
(NJDOE, 2011a).  Local school districts have been left
to implement strategies best suited to their student
populations (Mellard & Johnson, 2008).

The New Jersey Department of Education
created a system to measure all school districts socio-
economic status (SES) and educational
demographics. NJDOE (2011a) developed the district
factor groups to categorize school districts to measure
student performance with similar characteristics in the
state.  The categories were A (the lowest SES)
through J (the highest SES).  This system included
variables to measure the SES status of districts: (a)
percentage of adults without a high-school diploma,
(b) percentage of adults with some college education,
(c) occupational status, (d) unemployment rate, (e)
percentage of individuals in poverty, and (f) median
family income (NJDOE, 2011a).  The Sun Valley Lake
school district had a B rating (1990; 2000).  The New
Jersey Supreme Court in *Abbott v. Burke* (1981) ruled

Sun Valley Lake and 30 other New Jersey school districts students were not receiving the same economic and educational opportunities as their suburban counterparts. The New Jersey Report Card stated 65.7% of Sun Valley Lake third graders did not meet the proficient benchmark of NCLB in literacy (NJDOE, 2011c). To raise the literacy of struggling third-grade, African-American students, Sun Valley Lake implemented an intervention called the Success Program. The three-tier structure of the Success Program was modeled after the RTI model, which had realized positive results in elevating literacy of at-risk students (Miller, 2010; Vellutino, Scanlon, Zhang, & Schatschneider, 2008).

The purpose of this research study was to determine the relationship between participation in the Success Program and literacy test scores of African-American, third-grade students of the Sun Valley Lake school district. In this research study, the literacy of the participants was measured with four dependent variables: reading comprehension, oral reading fluency, instructional reading level, and sight-word recognition.

In this study, the researcher evaluated the efficacy of the Success Program in raising literacy scores of third-grade, African-American students. Knowledge about the efficacy of this program could have resulted in positive social change either through suggesting wider spread implementation of the program if it was successful or using a different program if it was not effective. Students reading on grade level in the third-grade had a 75% graduation rate from high school (Hernandez, 2011) and were less likely to encounter the justice system (Harlow, 2003). The results of this study could be shared with 30 other Abbott school districts promoting the positive aspects of the Success Program. Other struggling districts could use the Success Program or its elements to elevate the New Jersey literacy test scores on the New Jersey Assessment of Stalls and Knowledge (NJ-ASK) state assessment for third-grade, African-American students. This intervention program could have been replicated in school districts with similar student backgrounds across the United States. Because the Success Program was modeled after RTI methodology, it could add to the body of literature on RTI.

In this chapter, the background, problem, and purpose of the current study pertaining to the elevation of literacy skills were described. The research questions and hypotheses driving the current research followed. The relevant theoretical underpinnings as well as the nature of the study were described. The definitions as they pertained to this study are clarified. The assumptions critical to the meaningfulness of this study were described. The researcher described the scope and delimitations, followed by the limitations and significance of this study. The chapter concluded with a brief summary.

## Background

In New Jersey there were 31 school districts that continued to struggle in achieving academic standards. Researchers (Teale, Paciga, & Hoffman, 2007; Vogel, Rau, Baker, & Ashby, 2006) and the U.S. Census Bureau (2010) suggested poverty may have been a contributing factor in low academic performance. In New Jersey, 6% (69,249) of European-American children lived in poor families compared to 27% (75,906) of African-American

children. In this research study, the researcher
focused on one of the 31 Abbott districts in the New
Jersey school district of Sun Valley Lake. Sun Valley
Lake was an urban district in the State of New Jersey
that continued to struggle, educationally as well as
economically. The Sun Valley Lake school district
was categorized in the District Factor Group B, which
was the second lowest classification. NJDOE (2011a)
cited this school district for low academic
performance, particularly in literacy of African-
American students.

The administration of the Sun Valley Lake
school district received funding to initiate a program to
address low academic performance in the area of
literacy in African-American, third-grade students.
This early intervention literacy program, named
Success, was implemented during two consecutive
school years (2010-2011 and 2011–2012) in the
district's 10 elementary schools. All third-grade
students were given the Developmental Reading
Assessment (DRA) to assess fluency, comprehension
and instructional reading level, and the Dolch Sight-
Word List to assess the number of words students
recognized by sight. These two pre-tests were used

to identify third-grade, African-American students who were at least one full grade below third-grade reading level and were thus eligible for the Success Program. Identified African-American students were referred by their classroom teachers.  In each school year, there were two groups of 50 third-grade, African-American students reading at least one grade below the third-grade level.  The comparison group of 50 students were eligible for the Success Program, but there were not enough available spaces for these additional students needing assistance to have received the intervention.  The participant group of 50 students received the intervention program.

The Success Program was conducted as a pull-out intervention twice weekly for 40 minutes during the regular school day.  Two instructional support teachers provided supplemental literacy support over 35 weeks (beginning in the fall (2010) and continuing through the spring (2012).  The results of the Success Program intervention were measured with four dependent variables: reading comprehension, oral reading fluency, instructional reading level, and sight-word recognition.  Using archival data, the researcher addressed a portion of the district's struggling African-American students who had literacy deficits by assessing the relationship between participation of the third-grade students in the Success Program and improvements in literacy.

Extant data had not been analyzed to establish whether significant literacy was realized in the Success Program for third-grade, African-American students. This study was needed to determine if the Success Program was a course of action to address the literacy deficits of students in Sun Valley Lake. NJDOE has informed Sun Valley Lake there were a disproportionate number of African-American students, particularly in the elementary grades, who were not meeting the proficient academic benchmarks. With this study, the researcher evaluated a program with potential to improve the literacy of struggling third-grade, African-American students immediately and in the future.

## Problem Statement

Historically, policy and law had been enacted in an effort to ensure high educational standards in the United States. The No Child Left Behind act (NCLB;

2002) act was perhaps the most significant and far-reaching education policy initiative in the United States. This legislation expanded federal influence over the United States' more than 90,000 public schools. The No Child Left Behind regulation reauthorized the Elementary and Secondary Education Act (ESEA) to extend the historically restricted choice and scale of federal involvement in K–12 schooling (Dee & Jacob, 2011).

More schools must implement assorted programs to address academically struggling students with minimal additional funds. The 31 Abbott School districts struggled to understand federal regulations and bureaucratic rules. For local policy-makers, this mandate created some practical challenges, particularly in meeting a responsibility to set education policy and ensure instruction was both effective and financially efficient (Williams, 2011). School accountability was based on measuring each school's success in educating its students. The primary measure was progress toward literacy standards determined by state assessments.

In New Jersey, third-grade was the first-year students are tested to determine if they met NCLB benchmarks in literacy. In 2010, New Jersey's third-grade students' literacy was measured by the NJ-ASK. According to the New Jersey Report Card, 66.5% of all third-grade students scored proficient on the NJ-ASK (NJDOE, 2011). In Sun Valley Lake, the 2010 NJ-ASK third-grade literacy test scores reported only 34.3% of students attained the proficient benchmark. A student who scored a proficient rating was reading at grade level or higher (NCLB, 2002). Using archival data, the researcher investigated the results of the Success Program conducted in the Sun Valley Lake district during the 2010-2011 and 2011–2012 school years to address low-performing, third-grade, African-American students' literacy test scores.

Third-grade was a pivotal year in the education process. Students continued to explore literacy as they learned to read and comprehend. This foundation was critical because in fourth grade students were expected to read to expand their knowledge and critical thinking skills. As much as 50% of fourth grade curriculum could be incomprehensible to students below grade level in reading (Schorr & Marchand, 2007). Schorr and Marchand (2007) found readers measuring below proficient in third-grade remain below proficiency reading level in high school. Low academic performance was a precursor for behavior and social problems, as well as retention in later grades (Hernandez, 2011). Graduation rates could have been predicted based on student reading levels in the third-grade (Snow, Burns, & Griffin, 1998). Those students not reading proficiently in third-grade were four times more likely not to obtain a high-school diploma (Annie E. Casey Foundation, 2012; Hernandez, 2011).

Located in central New Jersey, Sun Valley Lake Public School District was an economically-challenged urban district. According to the National Center for Educational Statistics (2012), Sun Valley Lake public schools had 6,460 children enrolled, 76.8% of whom are eligible for a free or reduced-price lunch, indicating students and their families were living below the poverty guidelines according to the United States Department of Housing and Urban Development (2012). Nearly 14% of the residents of the school district were unemployed (U.S. Census Bureau, 2012). Sun Valley Lake spent $23,793 per pupil in 2012 annual expenditures (New Jersey Data

Bank [NJDB], 2012). In 2010-2011 and 2011-2012 school years funding had been reduced 27.1% (NJDB, 2012). Yet the 2013–2014 proposed school budget for Sun Valley Lake, one of the poorest districts in the state, suffered the largest dollar loss of all districts in its county (NJDB, 2012). According to NJDOE (2011a), the state's average cost per student in 2010 was $17,352. Pupil expenditures varied across the state, as noted by the NJDOE (2011b), from the lowest of $12,146 (Rockaway Boro) to the highest of $40,152 (Avalon Boro). Pupil expenditures of five random Abbott classified districts in 2010 included the following: Asbury Park $39,149l; Newark $27,498; Camden $28,456; Trenton 26,805; and Atlantic City $26,389 (NJDOE, 2011b).

This research study may contribute to the academic literature on reading skills for third-graders because there had not been any published studies conducted on third-grade, African-American students who participated in the Success Program in Sun Valley Lake. Sun Valley Lake, as well as the 30 other Abbott districts, could potentially use the results of this research study to evaluate a program that addressed the deficiency of supplemental early literacy. Addressing NCLB's expectation of third graders attaining proficiency on the state exam in literacy was critical as well. This research study could potentially change the way struggling, third-grade, African-American students were engaged in literacy in a supplemental literacy program that could have been replicated by school districts with characteristics similar to those found in Sun Valley Lake.

## Purpose of the Study

The purpose of this quantitative research study was to investigate the effect of the Success Program on the reading performance of Sun Valley Lake African-American students in third grade. The Success Program had two groups – 100 students who participated in the program and 100 students who did not participate in the program. The Success Program was conducted during two consecutive school years with 100 students in each year. The independent variable was the Success Program with two groups – 50 students who participated in the program and 50 students who did not. The Success Program was a newly created endeavor, because NJDOE (2011a) cited the Sun Valley Lake school district for low-student performance on literacy test scores of African-American students, particularly in the third grade. The Success Program was implemented during the 2010-2011 and 2011–2012 school years. Archival achievement data collected during those times was used. Literacy was the dependent variable based on measures of reading comprehension, reading fluency, instructional reading performance, and sight-word recognition.

## Research Question and Hypotheses

The overall guiding research question, followed by hypotheses, was provided below.

Was there a difference in literacy between students who participated in the Success Program and students who did not participate?

The independent variable was the Success Program over a two-year period with two groups – 100 students who participated in the program and 100 students who did not participate in the program.

Literacy was the dependent variable based on four measures: three variables from the DRA (reading comprehension, reading fluency, and instructional reading performance) and one variable from the Dolch Sight-Word List (sight-word recognition). Data from the dependent variable instruments were obtained from pre- and post-tests. These instruments were used in this study because the Sun Valley Lake school board approved them for the 2010-2011 and 2011-2012 school years to measure literacy. The Success Program and the achievement instruments were described in detail in Chapter 3. Low-performing, African-American, third-grade students were of primary interest. Archival data for the 2010-2011 and 2011–2012 school years were used for the data analyses. Analyses were done separately for each year. The .05 level of statistical significance was used to test the null hypotheses.

**Hypothesis 1**

$H_0$: There is no statistically significant difference in reading comprehension between students who participated in the Success Program

and students who did not participate in the Success
Program, as reported by the DRA pre- and post-test
assessment tool.

$H_a$: Students who participated in the Success
Program are expected to achieve a statistically
significant higher score in reading comprehension
than students who did not participate in the Success
Program, as reported by the DRA pre- and post-tests
assessment tool.

## Hypothesis 2

$H_0$: There is no statistically significant
difference in reading fluency between students who
participated in the Success Program and students
who did not participate in the Success Program, as
reported by the DRA pre- and post-test assessment
tool.

$H_a$: Students who participated in the Success
Program are expected to achieve a statistically
significant higher score in reading fluency than
students who did not participate in the Success

Program, as reported by the DRA pre- and post-test assessment tool.

## Hypothesis 3

$H_0$: There is no statistically significant difference in instructional reading performance between students who participated in the Success Program and students who did not participate in the Success Program, as reported by the DRA pre- and post-test assessment tool.

$H_a$: Students who participated in the Success Program are expected to achieve a statistically significant higher score in instructional reading performance than students who did not participate in the Success Program, as reported by the DRA pre- and post-test assessment tool.

## Hypothesis 4

$H_0$: There is no statistically significant difference in sight-word recognition between students who participated in the Success Program and students who did not participate in the Success Program, as reported by the Dolch Sight-Word List pre- and post-test assessment tool.

$H_a$: Students who participated in the Success Program are expected to achieve a statistically significant higher score in sight-word recognition than students who did not participate in the Success Program, as reported by the Dolch Sight-Word List pre- and post-test assessment tool.

### Theoretical Framework for the Study

Vygotsky's theoretical research in learning was congruent with the essence of the Success Program (Kozulin, 2009). Vygotsky considered relationships, culture, environment, and assessment as a part of the intervention process (as cited in Korepanova & Saphronova, 2011). Vygotsky (1978) postulated the Zone of Proximal Development (ZPD) was a safe environment where a teacher could have built upon skills a student had learned by molding what the student was ready to learn, subsequently. This supportive environment encouraged students to

become increasingly independent (Kozulin, 2011;
Vygotsky, 1978). This learning process in Vygotsky's
ZPD aligned with the Success Program because they
were both grounded in assessment, culture, and the
environment of the students. This learning process
was evidenced in the Success Program through the
four measures of this study: reading fluency, reading
comprehension, instructional reading performance,
and sight-word recognition.

The concept of resilience was used to illustrate
how a segment of the student population coped with
stress in their lives, particularly in economically-
challenged children like those in the Sun Valley Lake
school district. Risk factors were those environmental
problems or issues that had potentially negative
effects. Sun Valley Lake, the setting of this study, was
a high poverty school district (NJDOE, 2012a). The
effects of poverty/low income on children's literacy
may have been accentuated by neighborhood and
family socio-economic poverty. In this study, the
researcher intended to determine the relationship
between participation in the Success Program and
literacy test scores of African-American, third-grade
students of the Sun Valley Lake school district.

The Success Program used a three-tier structure that aligned with the RTI model. The RTI model used three basic components—Tier 1, Tier 2, and Tier 3. In Tier 1, the students were assessed. Tier 2 included small group instruction for children who were struggling. The third Tier involved more rigorous strategies (e.g., fewer children in a group, daily one-on-one sessions). RTI included student data to implement appropriate instruction and intervention in each tier (Dunn, Cole, & Estrada, 2009). IDEA (2004) suggested RTI was a viable three-tier model of intervention for academic, as well as behavior concerns. The RTI model had realized positive results in elevating literacy of at-risk students (Vellutino et al., 2008). In Chapter 2, the researcher described the theoretical underpinnings of Vygotsky's theory, the concept of resilience, and the RTI model drove the research questions in the Success Program in more detail.

## Nature of the Study

In this quantitative research study, the researcher investigated whether African-American, third grade, students who participated in the Success

Program performed better on post intervention

measures of literacy than students who did not

participate in the program.  The independent variable

was the Success Program with two groups – students

who participated in the program and students who did

not.  Literacy was the dependent variable based on

measures of reading comprehension, reading fluency,

instructional reading performance, and sight-word

recognition.  The participants were selected using a

non-probability criterion sampling, which dictated a

quasi-experimental design using a pre- and post-test

method.  Using this approach allowed conclusive

statistics to serve as the basis for answering the

research questions in this study.

The Success Program included two

assessment tools, the DRA and the Dolch Sight-Word

List, to assess students' literacy skills.  The

interventionist who supervised the program collected

and stores the assessments.  Archival data on

students in the Sun Valley Lake School District

participating in the Success Program for the 2010-

2011 and 2011–2012 school years were used for the

analyses. In Chapter 3, the researcher addressed the

methodology used to examine the research questions as well as the hypotheses.

## Definition of Terms

*Adequate Yearly Progress (AYP):* No Child Left Behind act (NCLB; 2002) expected all school districts to ensure 95% of their students attain pre-determined proficiency benchmarks. School districts were expected to make AYP toward these benchmarks. Failing to meet AYP for two consecutive years identified a school as needing improvement. There are penalties and sanctions determined by law for schools that did not make improvement and continued to fall short of AYP benchmarks (Children's Defense Fund, 2012b).

*Developmental Reading Assessment (DRA)*: The DRA was an instrument that provided information to educators regarding students' strengths and weakness in the areas of reading comprehension, oral reading fluency, and instructional reading level (Pearson Education, 2009).

*Dolch Sight-Word List*: The Dolch Sight-Word List comprised five lists totaling 220 words, which represented over 50% of the words used in the fourth-grade textbooks. The lists were *pre-primer* (pre = kindergarten), which consisted of 40 words a student should recognize before entering kindergarten; *primer Sight-Word List* (kindergarten), an additional 52 words students should recognize before entering first grade; *first grade Sight-Word List,* an additional 41 new words students should recognize before second grade; *second grade Sight-Word List,* which introduced an additional 46 words a student should recognize before entering third grade; and the *third-grade Sight-Word List,* which introduced an additional 41 words students should recognize before the end of third grade. There were an additional 41 words for third graders to learn before the end of the year (Meadan, Stoner, & Parette, 2008).

*Instructional reading performance*: For the purpose of this study, instructional reading performance was the students' ability to decode multi-syllabic words (Duran, 2003). The number of words in a timed-reading passage a student was able to recognize without difficulty was measured by the DRA.

*Intervention and referral service:* The intervention and referral service was a team of school professionals who suggested resources to address and provide resolutions for issues impeding the academic progress in general-education students (NJDOE, 2011a).

*Literacy:* For the purpose of this study, literacy was determined by reading comprehension, oral reading fluency, and instructional reading level based on the DRA, and sight-word recognition based on the Dolch Sight-Word List.

*Low-level skills:* Reading at the lowest level was the combination of three different skills often described as mechanical or low-level skills. These skills were the elementary operations that enabled the reader to decode the reading input (Troschitz, 2009).

*Micro-skills*: Micro-skills contrasted with the low-level skills, intellectual operations. They can be subdivided into two groups: *word recognition* and *understanding of syntax* (Troschitz, 2009).

*National Assessment of Educational Progress (NAEP)*: The National Center for Education Statistics conducted the NAEP. The NAEP reported student academic achievement nationally in core subjects as well as the arts (Children's Defense Fund, 2012b).

*National School Lunch Program*: In 1946, the Truman administration enacted a federal lunch program for students in public and private non-profit schools, as well as child-care centers. The guidelines stated students who resided in homes with incomes at 185% or less of the poverty level were to receive reduced-price lunch. Students who resided in homes with income at 130% or less of the poverty level were to receive free lunch. (NJDOE, 2011a).

*New Jersey Assessment of Stalls and Knowledge (NJ-ASK)*: A standardized test that measured student achievement in the knowledge and critical thinking skills required to proficient on grade level by the New Jersey Core Curriculum Content Standards in language arts literacy, math, and science. Tests were administered to students in Grades 3, 4, 6, 7, and 8 (NJDOE, 2011a).

*No Child Left Behind Act (NCLB)*: NCLB was a revision of the 1962 ESEA, initiated under President John F. Kennedy. When the Elementary and Secondary Education Act of 1965 (ESEA) was reauthorized in 2001 by the Bush Administration, it was renamed and amended to include components in reading literacy education, computer technology, and geography scores (Children's Defense Fund, 2004).

*Oral reading fluency*: Oral reading fluency was determined by intonation well as how smoothly and fluidly a text was read (Pearson Education, 2009).

*Quality Single Accountability Continuum* (QSAC): NJQSAC was NJDOE's (2011a) monitoring and evaluation system to measure NCLB in each school district.

*Reading comprehension*: The capability of a reader to make inferences and apply them in a meaningful way that demonstrated knowledge and understanding of meaningful text (Pearson Education, 2009).

*Response to Intervention (RTI)*: A model that used three basic components – Tier 1, Tier 2, and Tier 3. In Tier 1 the students were assessed. Tier 2 included small group instruction for struggling children. The third tier involved more rigorous strategies (e.g., fewer children in a group, daily one-on-one sessions). RTI used student data to implement appropriate instruction and intervention in each tier (Dunn et al., 2009).

*Sight-word recognition*: Words the reader has committed to memory that did not require phonetic analysis (Meadan et al., 2008).

*Socio-economic status (SES)*: SES was determined by several factors, usually considering income, level of education, and occupation. For the purposes of this study if students received free or reduced-price lunch, their SES status was considered impoverished (Howard, Dresser, & Kunklee, 2009).

*Supplemental educational services*: Extra academic instruction provided to income-eligible students who attended a Title I School in Need of Improvement. This additional academic support in language arts literacy and math must have been provided outside of the regular school day.  The No Child Left Behind act required Title I schools that had not met AYP two years in a row to have provided SES.  The SES must have been chosen from the NJDOE (2011a) approved list of vendors eligible to provide enrichment.

## Assumptions

It was assumed the DRA and Dolch Sight-Word List assessments were reliable and valid instruments for measuring the current study's research variables.

## Scope and Delimitations

The scope of this study was one urban school district's third-grade, African-American, students over a two-year period of time.  During two consecutive school years, there were 200 participants: 100 who participated in the Success Program and 100 who did not participate in the Success Program. The criterion for participation in the study was a literacy level at least one grade level below the current grade.

## Limitations

A study limitation was the sample participants were referred by classroom teachers, making the selection process not completely random, which could create possible bias. Another limitation was this study has no mechanism to evaluate any functioning deficits of the participants in terms of whether they lack capacity or motivation to master the skills. There was no indication whether any students participating in the study received other assistance to raise their literacy skills. The use of archival data precluded addressing these limitations.

The sample population was relatively small and limited to African-American students. Although care should be taken when generalizing the findings, it was probable the conclusions could have been generalized to wider populations with the same environments (e.g., poverty, low-literacy test scores). In New Jersey there were 30 additional Abbott-designated school districts with similar characteristics of this research study. Nationally, there are cities with African-American populations living below the poverty level with low-literacy test scores.

## Significance

Scholars had contributed to the literature on educational challenges faced by African-American students (Blanchett, Mumford, & Beachum, 2005; Cullinan & Kauffman, 2005; Ebersole & Kapp, 2007; Gardner & Miranda, 2001; Harry & Anderson, 1995; Harry, Klingner, & Hart, 2005; Hart, Cramer, Harry, Klingner, & Sturges, 2010; Hosterman, DuPaul, & Jitendra, 2008; Irving & Hudley, 2005; Jones & Menchetti, 2001; Kearns, Ford, & Linney, 2005; Lo & Cartledge, 2006; Olmeda & Kauffman, 2003); however, research was needed to determine the relationship between students who did not participate and students who participated in the Success Program and literacy test scores of African-American, third-grade students of the Sun Valley Lake school district. Research was required to determine strategies to improve the literacy of struggling African-

American students.  This research study had the potential to contribute to positive social change by filling a gap in the literature by evaluating the effectiveness of the Success Program.  No research conducted in Sun Valley Lake on African-American students in third-grade regarding literacy in terms of literacy test scores had been conducted to this researcher's knowledge, nor academically published. This study's findings may have contributed to the existing knowledge base by reporting the impact of a program designed to improve literacy by the end of third grade.  Students not reading proficiently in third-grade were four times more likely to fail to obtain a high-school diploma (Hernandez, 2011).  A lack of a high-school diploma may have lessened a person's opportunity for financial stability after graduation.

The purpose of this study was to determine if the Success Program was a positive intervention in increasing the literacy scores of third-grade, African-American students.  Determining whether the program was successful could have helped the administration justify why resources should have been reallocated for this research.  This research study added to literature for evidence-based programs.

## Summary

The administration of Sun Valley Lake was
interested in whether the Success Program was
successful and welcomed empirical research to
quantitatively confirm this determination. In this study,
the researcher used archival data from the 2010-2011
and 2011–2012 school years to determine whether
the students who participated in the program
performed better academically than students who did
not participate in the program. There had been
studies published on several of the larger (population)
Abbott school districts, but the researcher found no
published study with regard to approaches that may
have improved literacy of third-grade African-
American students in the Sun Lake Valley.

This study had the capacity to contribute to the
field of psychology because it would have filled a
knowledge gap existing since the State Supreme
Court of New Jersey issued the Abbott v. Burke
(1981) ruling that African-American children were not
receiving adequate education in 31 school districts.
Sun Valley Lake was one of these 31 special-needs

districts. NJ-ASK test scores were evidence that Sun Valley Lake students were still educationally challenged.

The barriers to literacy, including the impact of poverty as well as solutions, were elaborated in detail in Chapter 2.

## Chapter 2: Literature Review

## Introduction

Since the inception of NCLB, school districts have been held accountable for students achieving grade level literacy standards (Fernandez, 2009). The purpose of this study was to evaluate the effectiveness of a district-wide program designed to elevate the literacy scores of third-grade, African-American students. The Success Program was intended to provide reading skills to students who were at least one grade level below the expected proficient benchmark established by NCLB (2002). NCLB expected all third-grade students would be proficient by 2014. Even though NCLB did not require the use of RTI, it was cited as a positive intervention to address the literacy concerns of struggling students. This research study's setting was a Title I school district with documented low SES, low literacy test scores, and high poverty.

The researcher reviewed the literature related to literacy achievement in low-SES districts with large African-American populations. The theoretical framework of Vygotsky's (1978) theory of ZPD, which included scaffolding and small group instruction, was the cornerstone of this study's literacy intervention driving the research questions. In this chapter, the researcher described the conceptual framework of the resiliency theory. Resiliency, poverty, and literacy were examined as they pertained to study participants. The chapter then included a brief historical overview of literacy. The recent legislation regarding NCLB as it pertained to New Jersey was reviewed. Literacy in early elementary schools was discussed with the literacy challenges in New Jersey. The intervention to address the challenges of literacy in one district in New Jersey was the next section, which included a discussion of the RTI model used for the current research study. This chapter continued with the issue of assessing literacy including the instruments and variables. The state assessment NJ-ASK was discussed, as well as the instruments used in this research study – the DRA2 and the Dolch Sight-Word List. The chapter then concluded with a summary reviewing the key concepts of the literature review.

## Theoretical Foundation

### Vygotsky's Socio-Cultural Theory

The field of educational psychology had been influenced by Vygotsky. According to Vygotsky (1978), even though biological factors comprised the essential precondition for elementary development to emerge, socio-cultural factors were crucial for the elementary natural developmental process to grow. Vygotsky argued for the individuality of the social environment and considered socio-cultural settings as one of the influential factors in the growth of higher forms of individual mental activity such as intentional memory, voluntary attention, logical thought, planning, and problem-solving (as cited in Turuk, 2008).

In the socio-cultural theory, Vygotsky (1978) concentrated on the transmission of cultural values, beliefs, and customs among social groups from one generation to other. According to Korepanova and Saphronova (2011), Vygotsky's (1987) theory was

49

grounded in social interface. Cooperative dialogues among children and more well-informed members of a society were essential for children to learn the ways of behaving and thinking that made up the culture of a community (Korepanova & Saphronova, 2011). Vygotsky theorized children would be able to excel if they were supported and guided properly by teachers, mentors, and peers (Berk, 2007).

Vygotsky viewed both instruction and assessment as indivisible from one another (as cited in Korepanova & Saphronova, 2011). If teachers wanted to assess children's academic performance, they should not have focused on testing their performance with the final achievement test. Contrary to this common practice, their real focus should have been on the various class activities students might have engaged in with the help of their teachers and classroom peers. Students were able to progress in the tasks presented to them with the help of others; they might also have been able to succeed in their future tasks without the help of others (Yildirim, 2008).

## Zone of Proximal Development

Vygotsky (1978) postulated the ZPD was a safe environment in which a teacher can build upon skills a student had learned by molding what the student was ready to learn. In this supportive environment, teachers encouraged students to become independent (Kozulin, 2011; Vygotsky, 1978). By applying the concept of the ZPD to the Success Program, teachers expected the presence of adult molding would have resulted in student literacy improvement. The Success Program used scaffolding through planned opportunities for students to collaborate with their interventionist and peers in a small group setting. The interventionist modeled the acceptable exchanges and responses. The students become more confident, which encouraged them to have built the student's literacy knowledge.

## Scaffolding

Scaffolding was a viable learning tool. Veerappan, Wei Hui, and Sulaiman (2011) explained scaffolding in the classroom was a process in which the students were provided a temporary framework for learning by the teacher. Once the scaffolding was performed, students were motivated and encouraged to develop their own inventiveness, inspiration, and creativity. As the students started gathering knowledge and boosting learned skills on their own, the essentials of the framework were dismantled. Veerappan et al. postulated the process was concluded once the lesson was completed in the classroom; the scaffolding was then removed in total, and students no longer required it. Scaffolding might have been considered as three related pedagogical scales:

- Supporting the students in different activities and skills and giving them a definite support structure for their cognitive development.
- Performing specific activities in the classrooms.
- Giving help and assistance in moment-to-moment interface (Veerappan et al., 2011).

The socio-cultural theory coupled with the concept of ZPD formed the theoretical foundation of scaffolding (Korepanova & Saphronova, 2011).

Scaffolding was a way of operationalizing Vygotsky's perception of working in the ZPD. There were three basic features that enhanced the educational scaffolding in its specific character: (a) the fundamentally dialogic character of the communication in which knowledge was constructed, (b) importance of the kind of activity in which knowledge was embedded, and (c) role of artifacts that mediated the knowledge (Veerappan et al., 2011). When scaffolding, teachers used the ZPD as the catalyst to gradually transfer responsibility for the tasks from the teacher to the students. The role of the educator further accentuated the association between the learner and the teacher in constructing the essential skills and knowledge.

Several cultural and economic realities ensured early on that urban low-SES children would have received less stimuli that prepared them for school than their middle-income suburban counterparts. The vocabulary of middle-SES 3-year-old children was typically 1,000 to 5,000 words, nearly 50% more than low-SES children (Howard et al., 2009). African-American students entered the educational process behind their European-American counterparts, and as

students got older the achievement gap widened.
Ready (2010) suggested childhood poverty was
affected by school-related failure of cognitive
development. In fact, third-grade middle-SES
students had acquired 5,000 more words than low-
SES students (White, Graves, & Slater, 1990). One
of the reasons for this occurrence was inconsistency
in learning environments, particularly between high-
and low-performing schools. Socio-economically-
deprived children were allocated to several different
programs and groups that provided restricted
opportunities and resources to learn (Ready, 2010).

Suburban families tended to seek educational
support for students. Johnson and Johnson (1999)
pointed out middle-class and suburban families had
and continued to use educational support services
such as Sylvan, Huntington, and Kumon learning
centers to ensure their children's educational success.
Teachers, parents, and students reaped benefits from
such programs, and there was a consequent
decrease in grade retention (Johnson & Johnson,
1999). These kinds of supplemental educational
supports were costly for children living in poverty.
However, Sun Valley Lakewa one of the 31 low-

performing Abbott districts slated to have received
additional funds to provide supplemental educational
services to its students to close the educational
achievement gap.

Sun Valley Lake was an urban district trying to
catch up from years of educational neglect.
Educational supplements were necessary to reducing
achievement gaps. In the fiscal environment, some
states had been forced to cut budgets and slash
education spending. New Jersey's Governor Christie
inadequately funded schools by $1.6 billion in the
2010-2011 school year (Gewertz, 2011). This
educational budget cut was enacted in spite of Abbott
legislation, which defined a school funding formula for
the 31 most disadvantaged school districts in New
Jersey. Attorneys representing the Abbott districts
sought a ruling from the State Supreme Court to
uphold the court order of the school funding formula
to provide additional funds for the 31 impoverished
school districts (Gewertz, 2011). The court's decision
on May 24, 2011 to increase funding to the 31 Abbott
districts by $500 million was a direct response to
Governor Christie's educational budget cut of $1.6
billion (Gewertz, 2011), but it came too late for

students to benefit from the ruling in the 2010-2011
school year.

The 31 Abbott districts were faced with ensuring
students attained proficiency on the NJ-ASK with $1.1
billion less than anticipated in their budgets. New
Jersey was not the only state facing budget deficits;
many school districts are faced with decreased
funding and had been forced to find research-based
strategies successful in improving student literacy.
Veerappan et al. (2011) proposed scaffolding as an
instructional method in which the instructor modeled
the preferred learning strategies or tasks and then
shifted the tasks to the students. This type of
interface was consistent with Vygotsky's belief the
majority of learning happens within a social paradigm
… not in isolation (as cited in Markova & Medvedev,
2010). This process emerged when interaction
occurred among students and teachers in the
classroom. Even though Vygotsky did not use the
term scaffolding, it was still similar to the theoretical
foundation of ZPD. Vygotsky defined the ZPD as the
space between the level of potential development as
determined through problem-solving under teacher
guidance and interaction and collaboration with more

capable student peers and actual development level of the learner as determined by independent problem-solving (as cited in Markova & Medvedev, 2010). In applying the concept of the ZPD to the program participation of the students, the Success Program teachers expected presence of an adult interaction partner might have influenced improvement in the students' literacy scores.

In the classrooms, scaffolding was considered as a process in which the students were provided a temporary framework for learning by the teachers. Explicit connections between the content and literacy goals for designing instruction among the students must have emerged as relevant for the student to benefit from cultural modeling. Risko and Walker-Dalhouse (2007) found sharing experiences and knowledge among small group, peers, community, and family helped students. Two fundamental components of culturally-approachable instruction emerged from cultural modeling. These included respect for cultural differences and viewing these differences as learning and teaching resources, rather than as deficits to have been surmounted. Cultural modeling helped to provide impartial and accelerated opportunities for learning for all students; however, it was mainly empowering for students who belonged to racial groups whose language and culture were not visible in the classrooms (Lindenberger, 2011). Within the context of the ZPD, students benefited from experiencing diverse cultures through scaffolding. During the scaffolding process, the educators had opportunity to model appropriate cultural interactions and responses in a safe small group situation. In the intervention program titled Start Instruction with Texts That Build Upon Your African-American students' Knowledge and Experiences, students were more involved when culturally authentic African-American texts were used (Risko & Walker-Dalhouse, 2007). Swain and Lapkin (2000) found the ZPD had assisted South Korean elementary students in achieving tasks (learning English). During each small group session, the instructor built upon the knowledge the students had learned earlier. The students engaged in ZPD realized greater vocabulary than students learning English who had not been exposed to ZPD (Risko & Walker-Dalhouse, 2007).

## Small Group Instruction

A component of Vygotsky's theory, as well as of RTI, was instruction of children in small groups (as cited in Samuels, 2008 and in Vellutino et al., 2008). Students in a small group may have been more inclined to ask questions than in a large classroom environment. Small group instruction was a component of the Success Program. The Success Program's premise was the segmented instruction of small groups will have helped emerging readers by providing opportunities to strengthen literacy skills for academic growth. In the Success Program, students received individualized attention and instruction that may not have been possible in a large group or classroom activities. It was also expected teachers in the Success Program might have been able to observe how individual students performed on tasks and how they interacted with other students (Wasik, 2008).

Small group instruction provided a unique learning opportunity. Tyner (2009) found small group reading instruction included effective assessments and a balanced instructional scheme (guided reading, phonics, and writing). Effective contextual reading and systematic word study was paced to the learning speed of individual students. This kind of teaching and learning was convenient when instruction was delivered in the smaller grouped teams and helped to meet the literacy needs of the students (Tyner, 2009). According to Wasik (2008), there were certain factors that should have been given consideration while teaching students in the smaller groups.

The current study was grounded in small group instruction. During small group instruction, meaningful relationships emerged, making the scaffold approach a natural progression within the ZPD. The students in a small group may have been more inclined to ask questions than in a large classroom environment. Vygotsky argued students did not learn in isolation (as cited in Miller, 2011). Assessments were used to address the levels of the students and the teacher built on strengths of the students while providing enrichment for weaknesses (Miller, 2011). Small group guidelines mean that ...

- Groups should not exceed more than five children.
- Groups should be deliberately organized.

- Groups should be unique from center time
  activities.
- Groups can show better results than the whole
  groups to teach content if the schedules are
  rotated properly among students (Wasik, 2008).

According to Fien et al. (2011), progressive
instruction in the small group setting provided the
environment for students to have been immersed in
vocabulary and fluency, as well as the word meanings
and the words' applications. This small group
progressive instruction had the potential to reduce the
vocabulary achievement gap for students, as well as
comprehension challenges (Fien et al., 2011).

**Response to Intervention**

RTI had been implemented in school districts to
increase the opportunities and learning capabilities of
struggling students. This model had achieved
recognition in the United States in recent years
because it addressed the mandates of NCLB by
supporting struggling students, with academic as well
as behavioral strategies who were under IDEA

(Samuels, 2008). IDEA (year) suggested RTI was a model of intervention before referral was made to a child study team (CST). The CST members decided if the student was a candidate for special education services. The RTI model included a focus on literacy in short periods of time (Greenwood et al., 2011). As Greenwood et al. (2011) articulated, there were three basic components of the RTI model – Tier 1, Tier 2, and Tier 3. The first strategy (Tier 1) included the assessments and probable alterations of the language arts program in a targeted classroom. Assessments ensured the literacy instruction delivered by the classroom teacher addressed the needs of the individual, as well as all the children in the classroom (i.e., children who experience early literacy difficulties). The second strategy (Tier 2) includes the secondary (small group) instruction for children whose literacy difficulties were not resolved by suitable adjustments to the classroom instructional program. The third (Tier 3) involved more rigorous strategies (e.g., fewer children in a group, daily one-on-one tutoring). All three strategies relied on monitoring each student's progress as a basis for defining eligibility for the recommended tier of remediation. Furthermore, referral to a child study team, as well as diagnostic classification, was deferred pending the outcomes from the different tiers (Wanzek & Vaughn, 2010).

Vygotsky's learning process manifested in the RTI model of intervention. In Tier 1 the RTI model was congruent with Vygotsky's concept in the initial assessment of the student transpired through the relationship with the educator. Vygotsky's ZPD was centered on small group instruction, as was Tier 2 of the RTI model. Both Vygotsky and RTI expected the instructor to build upon a student's current knowledge base in small increments. Through modeling and encouragement, it was expected the student will have realized independence as confidence was gained (Bacon, 2005).

Although the literacy strategies and progress monitoring for struggling readers of the RTI model were fleshed out, questions persisted about how RTI could have fit into other subjects and with older students (Samuels, 2008). Vellutino et al. (2008) argued RTI models were based on work with reading-impaired children highly favored small group instruction as a major strategy to have improved literacy skills. The Success Program implemented strategies to improve literacy through small group instruction basing its structure on the RTI model.

## Conceptual Framework

## Resiliency

Social scientists had been concerned with the determinants of adverse social phenomena, such as interpersonal conflict and depression, on individuals who had little apparent capacity to shape these outcomes. In the 1970s, the research began to shift to focus on understanding why some persons succeeded in spite of adverse circumstances. This change in focus gave rise to studies on what was referred to as resilience, which had predominantly focused on characteristics of the individual. For instance, a review of the evidence showed since the 1970s children raised in deprived and adverse environments went on to become successful and loving individuals (Sirvani, 2007).

Resiliency's historical conceptual underpinnings were grounded in ecological systems. In ecological sciences, resilience related to the property of the ecological systems at different scales rather than populations.  There has been a significant evolution of the concept of resilience in ecology over the past decade in terms of its measurement and in terms of understanding how resilience interacting with other system properties such as diversity and stability (Powers, 2010).

The concept of resiliency had evolved in the social sciences as encompassing the capability to bounce back effectively regardless of the exposure to severe risk (Ross et al., 2008).  Student resiliency was fostered by environment where the student felt cared for and safe to explore academically (Ayalon, 2007).  At least one adult must be included who knew the child well and cared sincerely about the child's success (Ayalon, 2007).  Student resiliency could have also been enhanced through persistent support and high expectations, as well as opportunities for significant involvement (Ayalon, 2007).  Resilience included several environmental stresses such as poverty (Atkinson, Dietz, & Neumayer, 2007).

Resilience was therefore defined as interaction between humans and nature; the resilience of the

socio-ecological system was a central objective of
sustainability. Social elements of these systems
included the well-being and the governance of access
and regulation to resources in question. The
resilience of institutions depended on historic
evolution and inclusivity or exclusivity and how
effective institutions were in meeting the needs of a
segment of the society (Sirvani, 2007).

In the context of the present study, resilience
was anchored between a student's home and school
environments. Slavin, Lake, Davis, and Madden
(2008) indicated the failure of students to read at
grade level was not random, but concentrated among
schools serving low-SES minority students. In fact,
Bhattacharya, Currie, and Haider (2006) and
Fernandez (2009) documented the link between
student poverty, socio-economic status, and low
academic performance. The gap in performance
between children of different ethnic groups first
appeared in early elementary grades (Bhattachana et
al., 2006; Fernandez, 2009). This gap was perhaps
one of the most important policy issues in education
in the United States (Slavin et al., 2008).

Academic resilience was based on the general definition of resilience. Much of the resilience research included and went beyond literacy (Unger, 2010). Several researchers (Ayalon, 2007; Downey, 2008; Powers, 2010) looked at resilience as a broader concept encompassing physical, mental, and emotional health. Resilience was generally defined as the capacity to overcome, or the experience of having overcome, deleterious life events (Meece, 2010).

Recent research (Ayalon, 2007; Meece, 2010) on low-SES minority elementary students indicated the most powerful school characteristics for promoting resiliency (academic success) included a supportive school environment model that was safe and promoted positive student relationships. Downey (2008) noted in the resiliency model one educator was the pivotal person who know the child well and cared sincerely about the child's success. Ayalon (2007), Powers (2010), and Downey concluded students in these safe and nurturing environments displayed greater engagement in academic activities, a stronger sense of efficacy, higher self-esteem, and a more positive outlook toward school.

Compensatory strategies were tactics used by educators to assist students to overcome vulnerabilities or risk factors.  Morales (2008) and Ungar and Lerner (2008) indicated a number of factors were central to children's learning.  Benard (2004) and Henderson and Milstein (2003) found more instruction produced more learning.  Luthar, Cicchetti, and Becker (2000) examined the literature of resilience for conceptual and methodological weaknesses and noted research on resilience was an evolving approach which emerged in the 1970s focusing on internal (self-esteem), advanced to external (social environment), and more recently environmental factors, all of which linked with adaptation to perceived risk.  Perceived risk could be subjective in the research process.  Luthar et al. found resilience research lacked standards or a consensus of definitions and terminology.

The resiliency theory was a strengths-based construct grounded in the process of assessment, engagement, and intervention (Benard, 2004).  The current study aligned with this view and benefited from this theoretical approach.  This research study assessed student literacy which used two

instruments, the DRA and the Dolch Sight-Word List.
In terms of building relationships and fostering
engagement as part of the Success Program,
teachers were hired to provide literacy instruction to
the participants in safe, small group environments. As
the resiliency model suggested, this environment
provided students a safe atmosphere and encouraged
them to ask questions they may not have asked in the
classroom. The premise was, through the
intervention process, the student will have gained the
confidence to attempt to use newly acquired skills.

## Resiliency and the Impact of Poverty on Literacy

The rate of childhood poverty in the United
States had increased (U.S. Census Bureau, 2010).
The national rate rose from 15% in 2009 to 15.1% in
2010 (U.S. Census Bureau, 2010). The U.S. Census
Bureau (2012) reported 9,880,000 residents were
living below the poverty level in 2011. This growing
economic instability was reflected in the jump in the
number of children living in families receiving food
stamps. The number of children in families receiving
food stamps was 317,819 in 2010, up 58% from 2006

(Allen-Kyle & Parello, 2011). Allen-Kyle and Parello (2011) noted hungry children had more difficulty learning. By contrast when students were not hungry, there were fewer disciplinary referrals, fewer visits to the nurse, and greater student achievement (Allen-Kyle & Parello, 2011).

The landmark New Jersey Supreme Court case, Abbott v. Burke, established academic and social–emotional support for the state's 31 poorest districts to sustain early academic learning as a means of eradicating the effects of poverty. This ruling established there was a segment of students across the state who were economically vulnerable. The Abbott legislative order found students' achievement in school severely affected social and economic success as adults.

The structure and methods of the resiliency theory (Morales, 2008; Morales & Trotman, 2004; Ungar & Lerner, 2008) supported identifying common threads in improving the literacy achievement of at-risk African-American third-grade students. According to Morales and Trotman (2004), the resiliency model suggested the dynamics affecting at-risk students were protective factors, vulnerability areas, and compensatory strategies. The resiliency theory aligned with and supported illuminating the national (NCLB) and local (Abbott v. Burke) protective factors affecting the participants.

Risk factors were generally those environmental problems or issues with potential to place students in probable danger, such as lack of food and living in poverty. The protective factor directly affecting the current study on the national level was NCLB. The No Child Left Behind (NCLB; 2002) protected students' educational progress by ensuring students met pre-determined benchmarks. The No Child Left Behind (NCLB) act required school districts to achieve AYP, which meant schools must have produced annual incremental improvement in student's statewide standardized test scores (Department of Education, 2011). The No Child Left Behind act expected 95% of students to have scored proficient or above in statewide reading, math, and science tests by 2014. Even more directly protecting students in the Sun Valley Lake School District was the New Jersey Supreme Court decision Abbott v. Burke enacted to ensure the at-risk, poorest students in the state have the proper funding to support literacy.

Risk factors might have involved a culture of
violence, substandard schools, or lack of parental
consideration and interest. All of these factors were
probable to place a student at risk. Risk factors were
characteristics or features that worked to increase the
possibility of developing negative notions in an
individual (Powers, 2010). Conversely, protective
factors involved uniqueness and individuality, which
may have depicted optimistic encouraging effects on
outcomes and interact with risk factors that could
have altered or changed the impact (Powers, 2010).

African-Americans students living in poverty
areas were exposed to challenging life environments
that could have significantly hindered their goal
towards academic success. Burchinala, Vandergriftb,
Piantac, and Mashburnc (2008) and Downey (2008)
illustrated the higher risk factors of African-American
students in elementary and middle schools. The
multiple-risk model demonstrated by Burchinala et al.
recognized \there are several indices of risk – such as
poverty, single parenthood, large households, low-
parental education, unemployment, and low-income
communities and schools, and more proximal
measures such as maternal depression and lack of

social support that tended to cluster in the same individual.

School districts with high poverty rates had students with low literacy, which increased their susceptibility to experience factors such as low self-confidence and greater behavioral problems in the classroom (Bhattachana et al., 2006; Fernandez, 2009). According to Morales (2008), resilient students were able to do well in school while dealing with adverse situations such as severe poverty or learning deficiencies. In this research study, susceptibility to vulnerability manifested itself as students reading one grade level below what was expected in third-grade and the effect poverty may have had in this situation. The Success Program was a compensatory strategy that addressed the vulnerability of the participants in this research study.

Sun Valley Lake, high-poverty school district, had several environmental risk factors with potentially negative effects (NJDOE, 2012a). The effects of poverty/low-income on children's literacy may have been accentuated by neighborhood poverty. A holistic approach should be taken when identifying deficiencies in the academic performance of each student.  The holistic approach in determining academic performance was not limited to environmental risks, microsystem, and resilience. Correspondingly, research (Kim, Petscher, Schatschneider, & Foorman, 2010) on empirically supported intervention programs had revealed intervention across multiple domains suggested more resourceful than focusing on one aspect of a child's environment (Powers, 2010).  Swanson, Solis, Ciullo, and McKenna (2011), in their research on reading outcomes for at-risk early elementary students, found skill development should not have been concentrated in one specific area.  They found positive results when skills were developed across several domains: vocabulary, letter recognition, comprehension, and oral reading fluency through 'read-alouds' in small group instruction.  The research conducted by Swanson et al. aligned well with Sun Valley Lake's supplemental reading program.  The Success Program provided skill development as a collaborative intervention to African-American, at-risk, third-grade students during small group instruction in the areas of reading comprehension, oral reading fluency, instructional reading level, and sight-word recognition.

## Literature Review

## Historical Overview of Literacy

For a nation such as the United States to improve school literacy, it had to pay special attention to literacy achievement through third grade. Wilson and Colmar (2008) explained students who improved their learning ability in third-grade will have suffered fewer academic problems than students who failed to meet academic benchmarks in the third grade. According to Elias and Torres (2007), one out of six children faced reading and learning problems from Grades 1 to 3. Literacy not only related to reading, but was also considered the foundation of other areas of academic learning and application of education in life outside the school. Normally, students used reading skills for learning lessons, but when they struggled with literacy, they likely started to have difficulty in other academic sectors. Larson (2006) noted students who were not reading on the third-grade level by the end of the school year continued struggling in the remaining school years. Students

who read below grade level in the first grade but
received literacy intervention by and/or during third-
grade would have done well in their studies in high
school (Larson, 2006).

VanDerHeyden, Snyder, Broussard, and
Ramsdell (2007) recognized the increasing disparities
between purely school-based learning and literacy
practices in practical life. Educators could have
enhanced and mobilized students' knowledge and
performance by designing and redesigning textbooks
and syllabi with emphasis on social and real-world
importance. This sort of redesign effort would have
required textbooks applicable to the students' culture.
Educators may have found enhanced participation by
incorporating texts from relevant cultures, so students
will have paid special attention to the lesson (Larson,
2006).

## No Child Left Behind

The Department of Education had made
changes in the education sector in the last decade
(2002 -2012) and these changes affected goals and
provisions of education in public schools across

America (Ainsworth, Ortlieb, Cheek, Pate-Simnacher, & Fetters, 2012).  To fill the gap in education between poor and affluent students, one of the major goals of NCLB's framers was to provide education to minorities and economically challenged students to improve and develop their reading and writing skills. This act changed the environment of classrooms, schools, and literacy delivery.  The No Child Left Behind (NCLB; 2002) focused on five basic concepts or components:

- Linguistic and grammatical awareness
- Pronunciation ability
- Improvement in vocabulary
- Fluency in reading and speaking
- Comprehension (Ainsworth et al., 2012)

The No Child Left Behind act was the most significant and far-reaching education policy initiative in the United States.  This legislation stretched federal influence over the states' more than 90,000 public schools.  The No Child Left Behind act (NCLB; 2002) required each state to create a system of accountability applicable to all public schools and students.  These accountability systems included annual testing of public-school students in mathematics and reading in third-grade through eighth grade (Dee & Jacob, 2011).

## Literacy in Early Elementary School

The educational system must ensure students were able to read proficiently by the end of third grade.  Illiteracy impacted individuals, families and society as a whole.  The result of the 2003 National Assessment of Adult Literacy (NAAL) provided information on the future of our youth who did not attain the literacy benchmarks.  In it the National Center for Education Statistics (2003) reported two-thirds of the students not reading at grade level in fourth grade will have ended up on social service assistance or in a penal institution.  Harlow (2003) established a link between literacy and crime, noting 80% of the youth in the juvenile court system were functionally illiterate.  Harlow reported 70% of incarcerated individuals in the American penal system were reading at a fourth-grade level.  Some states used third-grade literacy test scores to project future inmate populations. Ensuring the reading comprehension of early elementary students will have benefited them immediately, as well as society in the future.

The vital importance of literacy in early elementary school, particularly in third grade, was well established. Children who fell behind their classmates in learning to read, not only have to catch up, but had to use their reading abilities to keep pace with the daily introduction of new lessons and skills (Gunn, Smolkowski, Biglan, & Black, 2002). Literacy was important for children at the elementary level, particularly as the academic environment became increasingly challenging in third-grade and children started to use skills for learning subjects like science, social studies, mathematics, and literature. Proficient literacy skills provided the opportunity to engage students in more intricate critical thinking and problem-solving tasks. Children who were poor readers at the end of first grade rarely attained average-level reading skills by the end of elementary school (Snow, 2005). Children who did not reach grade-level literacy skills, including writing and reading by third-grade, struggled to catch up in future

years. Snow (2005) found students who were poor
readers in third grade did not adequately develop their
reading and writing skills by the eighth grade.

## Literacy Challenges in New Jersey

Nationally NCLB policy makers had mobilized
an arsenal of policy instruments to ensure children
received a quality education to advocate for the
academic and social success of at-risk students
(Larson, 2006). New Jersey's children encountered
challenges that were not fully addressed in the NCLB
Act. The inequalities faced by students in New Jersey
required an additional protective layer NCLB had not
taken into consideration. The New Jersey Supreme
Court decision in Abbott v. Burke required significant
reforms and mandates for the state's poorest school
districts. To remedy the inequalities of school funding
and impact on the poorest residents of the state, the
New Jersey Supreme Court ordered an
unprecedented series of entitlements for urban school
children (Fernandez, 2009). These mandates
required per pupil spending be equalized between
urban districts and more affluent suburban districts.

The courts also ordered implementation of a series of specific standards-based education reforms for students in New Jersey for the 31 poorest districts in what came to be known as the Abbott remedies. These remedies contained a strong focus on assessment and data to close the achievement gap and instruction based on

- State core curriculum content standards
- Class-size limits
- Comprehensive literacy program from kindergarten through third grade
- Intensive and continual professional development
- Quality early childhood programs for all 3- and 4-year-olds (Fernandez, 2009).

**Literacy Interventions**

The three-tier approach of the Success Program was based on the RTI model, largely because it had proven effective (Greenwood et al., 2011; McGrath, McLaughlin, Derby, & Bucknell, 2012; Samuels, 2008; Vellutino et al., 2008) and could have been used to improve literacy achievement in elementary schools. The RTI model consisted of a framework that favored differentiating instructional strategies for individual students based on a demonstrated need. RTI was a method that used measurement, starting with a universal screening of the students (McGrath et al., 2012). Because students entered the Sun Valley Lake school district with limited exposure to early literacy experiences, all students were assessed with the DRA to determine their literacy level as part of Tier 1.

VanDerHeyden et al.'s (2007) research assessed Head Start preschool students using the Brigance Preschool Screen to identify lower performing students with greater risk of failure in the areas of letter naming and fluency. Using the RTI model VanDerHeyden et al. found students in the lowest 25% had the greatest improvement of skills whereas students in the highest 25% had the least improvement in skills. Students who responded to Tier 2 strategies were high responders. Wanzek and Vaughn (2010) evaluated third-grade students based on their reading skills. Based on these evaluations, the third-grade students were given Tier 2 small group instruction, resulting in positive outcomes.

## Assessing Literacy: Instruments and Variables

There was an urgent need for intervention and remediation for children below grade level in literacy. Scammacca, Vaughn, Roberts, Wanzek, and Torgesen (2007) suggested the focus of studies should have been on building emergent literacy that pointed toward the knowledge, skills, and approach considered developmental precursors in writing and reading. There were also several assessments in promoting the academic skills among the economically disadvantaged African-American students. Paris and Hoffman (2004) suggested rationales for these assessments lie in

- Research on reading development that indicated the importance of basic skills for future success.
- Classroom evidence that early diagnosis and remediation of reading difficulties could have improved children's reading achievement.

In response to NCLB's assessment requirements, NJDOE constructed an assessment.

The NJ-ASK was a state test for students in grades
three through eight. It was designed to give the
school information about how well the children were
achieving in the areas required by New Jersey's Core
Curriculum Content Standards. NJ-ASK was
administered to New Jersey's public-school students
in grades three through eight. Language arts and
mathematics were tested. In fourth and eighth
grades, science was also tested (Pizzo, 2008).

In third-grade, the New Jersey Common Core
Curriculum Standards placed emphasis on narrative
and expository texts, as well as literal and inferential
comprehension. In 2010, the NJ-ASK literacy test
was administered to third-grade students in the Sun
Valley Lake school district. The proficient rating
indicated a student was reading at grade level (NCLB,
2002). According to NCLB (2002), 95% of students
should read at grade level by 2014. According to the
New Jersey Historical Report Card Data 1995-2012
(NJDOE, 2012a), 66.5% of third-grade students
scored proficient on the NJ-ASK. In Sun Valley Lake
the 2010 NJ-ASK third-grade literacy test scores
reported 65.7% of students did not attain the
proficient benchmark.

Sun Valley Lake Public School District was an economically challenged urban district where 76.8% of the students were eligible for a free- or reduced-price lunch, which indicated they were living below the HUD poverty guidelines (Plainfield School District, 2011). A pre-ponderance of research literature (Hammer, Farkas, & Maczuga, 2010; Morgan & Meier, 2008; Wasik & Hindman, 2011) suggested poverty impacted language acquisition because children whose parents were professionals had larger vocabularies than children whose parents receiving Temporary Assistance to Needy Families (TANF). Hart and Risley (2003) found enormous differences in word exposure before age four, suggesting low-SES children were exposed to 30 million fewer words than medium- and high-SES children. Children residing in professional homes (middle class) had familiarity with or exposure to approximately 45 million words, whereas children residing in low-SES (TANF) homes had familiarity with or exposure to 13 million words (Champion, Hyter, McCabe, & Bland-Stewart, 2003). In terms of actual vocabulary by age 3, children whose parents were professionals had vocabularies of about 1,100 words and children whose parents

were TANF (social service) recipients had
vocabularies of about 522 words (Howard et al.,
2009). The Success Program was developed to
create opportunities to expand language acquisition.

**Developmental Reading Assessment**

The DRA was a set of independently managed
criterion-referenced reading assessments for students
in kindergarten through eighth grade. It was modeled
after a casual reading inventory and was used to
administer, score, and interpret the results by the
classroom teachers. DRA included two important
instruments involved in the DRA series. These
included Developmental Reading Assessment,
kindergarten through grade three, Second Edition
(DRA2), which included the DRA Word Analysis
(Weber, 2000), and the Developmental Reading
Assessment, grades four through eight, Second
Edition (Williams, 1999). The DRA2 K–3 and grades
four through eight were intended to identify students'
independent reading level, defined as a text on which
students met specific criteria in terms of accuracy,
fluency, and comprehension.

The DRA played a vital role in measuring progress of students as these measures were based on students' independent reading levels performance based on accuracy, fluency, and comprehension. The results obtained from DRA gave comparisons with respect to reading on grade level (Mullen, 2007). The Success Program used the DRA to assess the participants.

## Variables Measured by the DRA

**Reading comprehension.** Reading comprehension was the structure of the meaning of written communication through a shared, holistic interchange of concepts and ideas between an interpreter and the message (Rasinski, Brassell, & Yopp, 2008). The content of the meaning was affected by an interpreter's previous knowledge and experience. This definition suggested that reading comprehension needed an action on the part of reader. That action could have involved the use of prior knowledge the reader had on the topic of the text as well as the text itself to create meaning (Rasinski et al., 2008).

As early as possible, students should have begun working on a variety of comprehension skills, so they can continue reviewing skills and add new ones, learning as they grade transitioned. In third grade, emphasis was placed on narrative and expository texts, and literal and inferential comprehension (Duran, 2003). Students in third-grade continued using prior knowledge to answer questions, make connections with what they were reading, recalled major points made in the text, answered questions specific to what they have read, and searched for specific information in the text to answer questions about what they had read (Duran, 2003).

Reading comprehension was the ability to take information from written text, make inferences, and apply them in a way that demonstrated knowledge or understanding (Rasinski et al., 2008). Comprehension helped the reader to act on, respond to, and transform the information presented in written text that demonstrated understanding.

As reading skills were acquired, the ability to interpret underlying meanings, such as irony and sarcasm, was recognized as meta-linguistic

Read for Freedom: A Literacy Model to
Reduce the Next Generation of Prisoners

awareness. Meta-linguistic awareness in first grade was a statistically significant predictor of later reading-comprehension performance, when it was considered with academic aptitude (Duran, 2003). As late as third and fifth grade, meta-linguistic awareness still predicted reading-comprehension performance. Dreher and Zenge (1990) assessed the relationship between metalinguistic awareness in first grade and reading achievement in the third and fifth grades. The participants were randomly selected to participate in the study. The tests and procedures included standardized tests, interviews, and informal sessions. The results showed meta-linguistic awareness continues to account for at least as much variance in reading comprehension in the fifth grade as was identified in the third grade.

One of the significant components of education was learning to comprehend the meaning of texts. It was vital for students to know the significance of what they were reading or else the effort was pointless. Reading without comprehension was similar to talking to someone and listening without understanding.

As early as possible, students must have acquired knowledge of learning and literacy. This acquisition will have made the long-term educational process less arduous. Reading comprehension was significant for second and third-grade students. As Ari (2011) noted,


- It will make the life less problematic if children learned to comprehend what they read.
- Other than the knowledge of writing and reading, students should develop understanding of math, science, social studies, and other subjects as that understanding established the foundation for future education, thus making the learning experience well-rounded and measurable.
- It will have improved the vocabulary of the learners, which was a basic requirement of reading comprehension, and they will have gained confidence in writing and reading.
- They will have been able to read fluently, mimicking their normal speech patterns.
- It will have assisted students to relate to topics they were reading about to their life experiences or to earlier understanding from other texts.

To achieve these goals, it was important to introduce emerging readers to vocabulary, language, and reading opportunities early. Emerging readers' environment should have supported them in the progression of reading skills. When third-grade students enhanced their skills and had a better understanding of what they were reading, they discovered new knowledge and formed new strategies to build comprehension. Improved comprehension will have broadened students' horizons, opening a new world of reading (Rasinski et al., 2008).

The No Child Left Behind act (2002) required third graders be measured in reading comprehension. New Jersey used the NJ-ASK third-grade literacy test for this measurement. This study used third-grade reading comprehension as one of three distal measures assessed using the DRA instrument.

**Reading fluency.** Defining reading fluency was considered one of the most complex skills to attain. Fluency was an extremely difficult proficiency to acquire and involved quick and correct processing, which was conjointly intertwined with several skills

(Duran, 2003). Fluency entailed automatic
processing, the ability to smoothly read large
passages of reading, and incidental, or implicit,
learning (Duran, 2003).

Fluency was often defined as reading quickly,
smoothly, and with expression. For students to
become fluent readers, they must have been accurate
readers (Duran, 2003). Such a definition of fluency
included skills in rapid word recognition, rapid reading
rate, extensive exposure to print (large amounts of
reading), accuracy in comprehension, and
incremental learning (Rasinski et al., 2008). Fluency
was a skill to be mastered, but for students to
comprehend they must go beyond accuracy to
decoding (Duran, 2003).

Grabe (2010) proposed the amount of reading
was a strong predictor for good reading skills. He
conducted an international study that correlated the
relationship between amount of reading and
achievement for fourth-grade students. Grabe found
reading, use of language, word recognition,
vocabulary, and fluent use of language needed to be
reinforced.

Reading fluency had been a major concern of young readers' literacy development since it became one of the five pillars – along with phonemic awareness, phonics, vocabulary, and comprehension – of early reading education (Ari, 2011). Reading fluency, according to the NRP (2000), improved as accuracy was developed and subsequently reading had a natural flow. Fluency was usually measured as the number of words read correctly (orally or silently) per minute (Ari, 2011).

Several researchers consider students' level of fluency as directly related to comprehension skills. Kim et al. (2010) examined the relationship of growth trajectories of oral reading fluency, vocabulary, phonological awareness, letter-naming fluency, and nonsense word reading fluency from first grade to third grade. It was found oral reading frequency showed a relatively higher order reading skill (Kim et al., 2010). Pilonieta (2012) in an 8-week research study assessed reading rate, or correct words per minute, and concluded reading fluency was strongly related with reading comprehension. According to Kostewicz (2012), students practicing towards increased fluency rates not only build confidence, but also experienced other successful effects.

Reading fluency was important for students as it would have helped them to understand and articulate the main topics and themes of texts. For example, students might read a story about the sun as an introduction to the solar system and gain information such as how the sun benefited the earth, that it was a star, and how it rotated. This knowledge was building on existing knowledge such as its shape, that the sun produced light, and rose in the east and set in the west. Students would be able to connect this subject with their own life experiences (e.g., The sun was yellow and round. It rose in the morning.) and articulated their learning with others (Rasinski et al., 2008).

Reading, in a fluent manner, built confidence in students as reading increasingly mimicked normal speech patterns (Meadan et al., 2008). This research study used third-grade oral reading fluency as one of three distal measures assessed using the DRA instrument.

**Instructional reading performance.** Reading level depends on low-level skills and micro-skills. The purpose of reading instruction was to ensure students were ready to properly establish the words of a text and extract the correct meaning. By specializing in word-level signals, a reader will have recognized words while not being distracted by different stimuli, like pictures being presented within the reading context (Conley, Derby, Roberts-Gwinn, Weber, & McLaughlin, 2004). According to Duran (2003), as students progressed in word analysis skills, they encountered complicated words. Third-grade students were expected to learn ways to decode multi-syllabic words. They were taught to use structural options of such word elements as affixes (e.g., pre, mis, tion) to assist in word recognition.

## Variables Measured by Sight-word Recognition

Word recognition was an essential part of reading comprehension because it included processes necessary to give a word meaning and context (Troschitz, 2009). Understanding a sentence was more than substituting every given word or phrase with its translation. A reader must be able to understand the meaning of a word or phrase.

Language items developed meaning in context and understanding this meaning was called word recognition (Troschitz, 2009), which itself was a compound of different meanings (Troschitz, 2009). Sight-word recognition was defined as a discrete, observable response controlled by a printed stimulus (Meadan et al., 2008). Sight words were recognized without mediation or phonetic analysis, could be read from memory, and included not only high frequency words, but any words that could have been read from memory (Meadan et al., 2008).

According to Duran (2003), sight words were words not yet introduced as a part of the reading lesson when students encountered new sounds and syllables as a part of the original reading lesson. Most third-grade students were acquainted with sight words that helped them to become more fluent in reading. In addition to sight-word recognition, early readers sounded out unfamiliar words. Decoding was the process of phonetically sounding out words. It was necessary for students to acquire decoding skills. Decoding skills assisted students to read unfamiliar words easily by breaking them into parts. It also helped them to spell the words. When students were

able to read long sentences other than word by word
(Duran, 2003), it helped them to read independently
and understand more of what they were reading.

## Variable Measured by the Dolch Sight-Word List

Teaching sight words to third-grade readers
might require explicit skill instruction from education
professionals. One of the most frequently used lists
to teach sight words was the Dolch Sight-Word List
(Meadan et al., 2008) which included 220 words that
represented over 50% of words found in printed
material. If all of the Dolch sight words were
mastered, a learner would have been able to read at
a third-grade level. Realizing over half of third-grade
students in Sun Valley Lake were not proficient in
literacy, the Success Program implemented the Dolch
Sight-Word List as a literacy strategy.

There were five Dolch Sight-Word Lists. It was
expected each student would have been able to
recognize all of words before entering a subsequent
grade. The lists were preprimary (pre-kindergarten),
consisting of 40 words a student should have
recognized before entering kindergarten; primer

Sight-Word List, an additional 52 words that students should have recognized before entering first grade; first grade Sight-Word List, an additional 41 new words students should have recognized before second grade; second grade Sight-Word List, an additional 46 words a student should have recognized before entering third grade; and third-grade Sight-Word List, an additional 41 words that students should have recognized before the end of third grade.  There were an additional 41 words for third graders to learn before the end of the year.  This study assessed students' sight-word recognition with a pre-test and a post-test using the Dolch Sight-Word List for third-grade students.

## Summary and Conclusions

Research had clearly documented the existence of a literacy achievement gap between children of low-SES families living in lower-income urban communities and children of affluent higher-income families (Hart et al., 2010; Hosterman et al., 2008; Irving & Hudley, 2005; Jones & Menchetti, 2001; Kearns et al., 2005; Lo & Cartledge, 2006; Olmeda &

Kauffman, 2003). In terms of literacy, children from low-income families score on average 60% below children from higher-income families, and once the children from poverty fell behind, they tended to stay behind (Children's Defense Fund, 2004). Scholars determined reading comprehension, oral reading fluency, and sight-word recognition were major constructs to be considered in assisting students with elevating literacy levels (Ari, 2011; Grabe, 2010; Meadan et al., 2008).

Further research was required to determine what strategies worked and did not work for African-American students to improve their literacy skills. A gap in the literature existed because there had not been any published research conducted in Sun Valley Lake on African-American students in third-grade regarding literacy in terms of literacy test scores. This study's findings may have contributed to the existing knowledge base by reporting the impact of a program to improve literacy by the end of third grade. Students not reading proficiently in third-grade were four times more likely to fail to obtain a high-school diploma (Hernandez, 2011). Lack of a high-school diploma may have lessened a person's opportunity for financial stability. According to the Children's Defense Fund (2004), every year a child spends in poverty results in a cost of $11,800 in lost future production. A parallel existed between economic success and academic success (Children's Defense Fund, 2004); therefore, this study will have contributed to society's future citizens.

Veerappan et al. (2011) described scaffolding as the instructor modeling the preferred learning strategies or tasks and then slowly shifting learning tasks to students. This type of instruction seemed to be consistent with Vygotsky's belief learning was a social process and not an individual one, which emerged when interaction occurred among the students and teachers in the classroom. Even though Vygotsky did not use the term scaffolding, it still possessed a theoretical foundation in his discussion of the ZPD. He defined the ZPD as the space between the level of potential development, as determined through problem solving under teacher guidance, and interaction and collaboration with more capable student peers and actual development level of the learner, as determined by independent problem solving.

This researcher chose resiliency theory as the theoretical framework for the current study because this theory demonstrated individuals possess marked behaviors associated with optimistic performance (Benard, 2004). Resilience encompassed a number of elements, including environmental stresses such as poverty that warranted corrective action (Atkinson et al., 2007). This research study was intended to determine the relationship between participation in the Success Program and literacy test scores of African-American third-grade students of the Sun Valley Lake school district. The three-tier structure of the Success Program was modeled after the RTI model, which had realized positive results in elevating literacy of at-risk students (Vellutino et al., 2008). Chapter 3 described the research design, methods, and rationale providing a connection to the resiliency model, RTI, and the variables in this research study.

## Chapter 3: Research Method

## Introduction

Using archival data, the researcher evaluated
the effectiveness of the Success Program, a district-
wide initiative designed to elevate the literacy of third-
grade, African-American students reading below
grade level, conducted during the 2010-2011 and
2011-2012 school years. The Success Program and
assessments was conducted in the same manner
each school year. The purpose of this study was to
determine if the students who participated in the
Success Program (program group) had significantly
higher performance on measures of achievement
than similar children who did not participate
(comparison group) in the Success Program.

In this chapter, the research design and
rationale were discussed, including the variables. The
chapter included the methodology, sampling
procedure, characteristics exclusive to the population,

and a discussion of the data collection method and
the instruments used in the assessment of the
sample. This researcher also discussed threats to
validity, ethical procedures, and concerns regarding
data and the protection of participants' rights. The
chapter concluded with an overall summary of the
design and methodology.

**Research Design and Rationale**

This researcher used archival data collected
during the 2010-2011 and 2011-2012 school years to
determine whether the students who participated
(program group) in the Success Program performed
better academically than students who did not
participate (comparison group) in the Success
Program. The independent variable was the Success
Program with two groups – students who participated
in the Success Program and students who did not.
Literacy was the dependent variable, based on
measures of reading comprehension, reading fluency,
instructional reading performance, and sight-word
recognition. The participants were selected using a
non-probability criterion sampling, which dictated a

quasi-experimental design using a pre- and post-test method. Using this approach allowed conclusive statistics in response to the research questions in the current study.

The Success Program used two assessment tools, the DRA and the Dolch word list, to determine if students' participation elevated their literacy skills. These assessments were used in this study because the school district purchased and adopted the DRA2 and Dolch Sight-Word List instruments to be used district wide with all kindergarten through third-grade students. Therefore, no resource constraints were associated with the research design of this study. Both instruments aligned with the New Jersey Common Core Standards (NJCCS) as well as the curriculum used during the 2010-2011 and 2011–2012 school years. The district provided the staff with professional development in the administration and recording procedures of these instruments. Research designs using reliable data would have added to the knowledge base of elevating literacy skills in third-grade, African-American students in high poverty school districts.

# Methodology

## Population

The participants in this study totaled 200 students. There were 100 students per year for two years – 50 students (program group) who took part in the Success Program the first year (2010-2011) and a second group (comparison group) of 50 students who did not participate in the first year of the Success Program. Data collected for the second year (2011-2012) included scores of 50 students (program group) who took part in the Success Program and a comparison group of 50 students who did not participate in the Success Program. The criteria for participation in the Success Program was the students had to be in the third-grade and at least one grade level below their current grade in literacy as measured by the DRA2 and the Dolch Sight-Word List assessments. All of the participants of the Success Program were African-American. The comparison group met the same criteria as the participant group: Students had to be in the third-grade and at least one grade level below their current grade in literacy as measured by the DRA2 and the Dolch Sight-Word List assessments. The comparison group was 50 African-American, third-grade students from the same school years who met the same criteria, but who had not participated in the Success Program. Archival DRA2 and Dolch Sight-Word List records were available for both groups.

## Sampling and Sampling Procedures

This researcher used a non-probability criterion sampling method. This method was suitable because the researcher had criteria for each of the two groups. The participant group must have completed the Success Program. Only students meeting this criterion were accepted and included into the participant group for this study. The criterion for inclusion in the comparison group was they were academically eligible for the Success Program, but who did not participate. Students had to be African-American, in the third grade, and at least one grade level below their current grade in literacy as measured by the DRA2 and the Dolch Sight-Word List assessments.

## Procedures for Recruitment Participation and Data Collection

The Success Program participants were located at all 10 elementary schools in the district. The Success Program was conducted in the same manner each of the two years. In the beginning of each school year, the DRA2 and the Dolch Sight-Word List were administered in the third-grade classrooms as pre-tests. This test administration took place no later than the second week of October. For students to be considered a participant in the Success Program they had to meet the following criteria: (a) African-American, (b) in the third-grade during participation in the program (c) in a general education classroom and (d) at least one grade level below in literacy according to four measures: reading fluency, reading comprehension, instructional reading performance, and sight-word recognition. The comparison group was composed of students who met the criteria to participate in the Success Program, but whom did not participate.

Classroom teachers were asked to submit the names of students meeting the eligibility guidelines to the interventionist. The interventionist selected students from the classroom teacher recommendations for participation in the Success Program. There were 50 spaces for participation in the Success Program. Eligible students who were not placed in the Success Program due to limited space were placed in the comparison group. Parents were notified their child was receiving supplemental intervention during classroom literacy instruction. Parental consent was not required for participation in the Success Program.

The DRA2 and the Dolch Sight-Word List were administered no later than the second week of June to all third-grade students as post-tests. There were pre- and post-test scores available on all third-grade students for the school years 2010-2011 and 2011–2012. The test results were recorded in each student's permanent record. The interventionist who oversaw the Success Program also had a copy of the DRA and Dolch Sight-Word List test results for all students. The researcher used archival data to obtain the pre- and post-test scores for the program group students and the comparison group students.

The district's procedure to access these archival data was to request permission from the superintendent of schools, as well as the person directly responsible for the security of the scores (the letter of cooperation was located in Appendix A). To ensure confidentiality, the students were not identified by name or by the school of enrollment. All student data were coded before their test results were released to me. The analyses of the pre- and post-tests were based on aggregated data.

## Instrumentation

The DRA2, K–3 (Beaver, 2006) and the Dolch (1942) Sight-Word List were used as the measures of literacy by the school district. The DRA2 was used to measure reading comprehension, reading fluency, and instructional reading level and provides educators with information to implement instructional strategies (Williams, 1999). In 1996, a large formal field test was conducted with 84 teachers and 346 students in kindergarten through third-grade across 10 states and one province in Canada. The

sample was considered ethnically diverse, and 16%
of the participants were from urban areas. A nearly
equal number of male and female students were
assessed. During May and September of 2000,
additional field tests were conducted in 39 school
districts in the United States and two provinces in
Canada, encompassing 208 students in kindergarten
through third grade. Further field testing was done in
the fall of 2004 and the spring of 2005 and published
in 2006. Revisions were made based on the NRP
(2000) report and Reading for Understanding (Snow,
2002). Reliabilities (Cronbach's alpha) were greater
than .75, and concurrent validity was found when
correlated with the Iowa Test of Basic Skills (Williams,
1999).

The Dolch Sight-Word List was first
developed in 1936 and published as a test in 1942.
This list represents the expected vocabulary of
primary materials and encompasses over 50% of all
words used in schoolbooks and other publications
(preschool through third grade). The list consists of
service words, which are pronouns, prepositions, and
verbs not learned without pictures.

The school district adopted the DRA2 and
Dolch Sight-Word List instruments to be used district
wide with all kindergarten through third-grade
students. Both instruments aligned with the NJCCS
as well as the curriculum used during the 2010-2011
and 2011–2012 school years and continue to be used.
The district had provided the staff with professional
development in the administration and recording
procedures of these instruments.

## Operationalization for Each Variable

The objective of the analysis was to
determine statistically if there was a difference in
literacy between students who participated (program
group) in the Success Program and students
(comparison group) who did not participate. Archival
data for the 2010-2011 and 2011–2012 school years
were used. For purposes of the analysis, literacy was
operationally defined as the scores on the three
subscales of the DRA2 and the score on the Dolch
Sight-Word List. The .05 level of statistical
significance was used to test the null hypotheses.
Each of the four variables in this study was described

below with an operational definition, an explanation of how it was measured and scored, and an explanation of what the scores represent.

Oral reading fluency was defined by the NRP (2000) as accurate, rapid, and expressive reading. A student's score was contingent on how well oral reading fluency has been mastered in four categories: expression, phrasing, rate, and accuracy. For each of the four categories, a student received a numeric score from 1 to 4. Using the DRA, oral reading fluency was calculated by summing a student's scores, which indicates the child's ability. The lowest possible score a student could have received was 4 and the highest was 16. This score placed the student in one of four categories: intervention, 4–6; instructional, 7–10; independent, 11–14; and advanced, 15–16. In this study, student scores revealed an increase in literacy acquisition.

Reading comprehension could be defined as the ability to take information from written text and reiterate it in a way that demonstrated knowledge or understanding of that information (Rasinski et al., 2008). Reading comprehension needed action on the part of a reader. That action could have involved the use of prior knowledge the reader had on the topic of the text and the text itself to create meaning (Rasinski et al., 2008). A student's score was contingent on how well reading comprehension has been mastered. Student reading comprehension was calculated on the DRA using six categories: use of test factors, questioning/prediction, scaffold summary, literal comprehension, interpretation, and reflection. For each of the six categories a student received a score of 1 to 4. Comprehension was calculated by adding the student's score from each category, from 6 to 24, which indicated the child's ability. The lowest possible score a student could have received was 6 and the highest was 24. This score placed the student in one of four categories: intervention, 6–11; instructional, 12–16; independent, 17–22; and advanced, 23–24. In this study, success was achieved when a student scored in the independent or advanced levels.

A student's instructional reading level can be assessed by word recognition and understanding of syntax (Troschitz, 2009). When administrating the DRA, a third-grade student's instructional reading level was calculated by summing the student's scores (from 26 the lowest to 38 the highest), which indicated the child's reading ability. The student's score was contingent on the leveled reading book he or she was able to read with few errors.

Sight words are a list of words recognized without thinking or phonetic analysis (Meadan et al., 2008). Sight words are committed to memory and include not only high frequency words, but any words that can be read from memory (Meadan et al., 2008). There were five Dolch sight-word lists from pre-kindergarten through third-grade incorporated into the present study. The Dolch Pre-primer Assessment consisted of 40 words students should have known before entering kindergarten. The Dolch primer Sight-Word List consists of an additional 52 words students should have mastered before entering first grade. At the end of first grade, there were 41 new words students were expected to add to their vocabulary by the second grade. In second grade, students were introduced to 46 words to be memorized before entering third grade. There were an additional 41 words for third graders to learn before the end of the year. The words totaled 220, which comprised over 50% of the words used in fourth grade textbooks. The score was calculated using a worksheet for each grade level. If the child did not master all of the words on the worksheet, supplemental assistance was given. When a child begins kindergarten, 75 of the total 220 words should have been mastered. When a child began first grade, 120 of the total 220 words should have been mastered first. When a child began second grade, 170 of the total 220 words should have been mastered. When a child began third grade, 210 of the total 220 words should have been mastered. When a child began fourth grade, 220 of the total 220 words should have been mastered. Mastery was achieved when all 220 words are recognized by sight. Third-grade students were expected to reach mastery on the DRA post-test given at the end of the school year.

**Data Analysis Plan**

The data in this study were analyzed using the SPSS software program, Version 14.0 for Windows, analysis of variance (MANOVA). Prior to conducting the MANOVAs, the data were screened for outliers and the assumptions of normality, linearity, and homogeneity of variance. Any discrepancies were dealt with according to procedures suggested in the Publication Manual of the American Psychological Association (APA, 2010) and Statistics for the Behavioral Sciences (Gravetter & Wallnau, 2007).

The hypotheses associated with each of the achievement scales were as follows:

## Hypothesis 1

H0: There is no statistically significant difference in reading comprehension between students who participated in the Success Program and students who did not participate in the Success Program, as reported by the DRA pre- and post-test assessment tool.

Ha: Students who participated in the Success Program are expected to achieve a statistically significant higher score in reading comprehension than students who did not participate in the Success Program, as reported by the DRA pre- and post-tests assessment tool.

## Hypothesis 2

$H_0$: There is no statistically significant
difference in reading fluency between students who
participated in the Success Program and students
who did not participate in the Success Program, as
reported by the DRA pre- and post-test assessment
tool.

Ha: Students who participated in the Success
Program are expected to achieve a statistically
significant higher score in reading fluency than
students who did not participate in the Success
Program, as reported by the DRA pre- and post-tests
assessment tool.

## Hypothesis 3

$H0$: There is no statistically significant
difference in instructional reading performance
between students who participated in the Success
Program and students who did not participate in the
Success Program, as reported by the DRA pre- and
post-test assessment tool.

Ha: Students who participated in the Success Program are expected to achieve a statistically significant higher score in instructional reading performance than students who did not participate in the Success Program, as reported by the DRA pre- and post-test assessment tool.

## Hypothesis 4

H0: There is no statistically significant difference in sight-word recognition between students who participated in the Success Program and students who did not participate in the Success Program, as reported by the Dolch Sight-Word List pre- and post-test assessment tool.

Ha: Students who participated in the Success Program are expected to achieve a statistically significant higher score in sight-word recognition than students who did not participate in the Success Program, as reported by the Dolch Sight-Word List pre- and post-test assessment tool.

A multivariate analysis of variance (MANOVA) was the statistical procedure employed to test the null hypotheses (Gravetter & Wallnau, 2007). This procedure was used to test for a difference between the means on the post-tests, while statistically controlling for possible pretest differences. The reading comprehension, reading fluency, instructional reading, and sight-word recognition pretest scores were entered as covariates. If there were pretest differences between the two groups on any of the DRA2 scales or on the Dolch Sight-Word List before the Success Program was implemented, the post-test means were adjusted through the use of covariates to take the preprogram differences into account. The .05 level was used as the criterion for statistical significance.

Because there were four measures of literacy as represented by the four hypotheses, four MANOVAs were employed for each year the program was conducted, for a total of eight MANOVAs. Descriptive statistics (means and standard deviations) were reported as part of the MANOVA. MANOVA only provided information about statistical significance. It provided no information about how important the results may be.  Effect size, regardless of statistical significance, was an indicator of importance and was reported to accompany the statistical results (Gravetter & Wallnau, 2007).

## Threats to Validity

## External Validity

External validity impacts several aspects of the current study.  The pre- and the post-test were administered by a teacher who may have led the students or have had bias in scoring the tests.  The students may have been distracted or not felt well when the tests were administered. The researcher was not involved with the selection of participants nor with the administration of either assessment, and the researcher had no knowledge of out-of-school support the students may have been exposed to such as tutoring programs, educational television programs, reading books, or encouragement from their home environments.

## Internal Validity

Internal validity in terms of maturation was anticipated as a natural progression in the study participants. Third-grade students may have performed in a positive or a negative manner in response to a relationship developed with the interventionist. The assessment instruments in this study (DRA2 and Dolch Sight Word) had been determined to be statistically valid. Sun Valley Lake school district had found these assessment instruments appropriate to address the impact of the Success Program on literacy test scores.

## Threats to Construct or Statistical Conclusion Validity

Because the study used archival data and was limited to 50 participants for each group (participant and comparison) per year, the statistical power may have been low and influenced the statistical conclusion validity resulting in Type II error. As such, power for different effect sizes was determined and reported as part of the analysis.

Regardless of statistical validity, effect sizes were also reported as described in the Publication Manual of the American Psychological Association (APA, 2010). Effect size was an indicator of the magnitude or the importance of a result, irrespective of statistical significance (Gravetter & Wallnau, 2007).

**Ethical Procedures**

Permission to conduct this study using archived data needed to be granted by the superintendent of schools. The letter of cooperation was located in Appendix A. The interventionist provided the pre- and post-test results of two assessments, the DRA and the Dolch Sight-Word List to the researcher in an anonymous format. The students were identified by two initials. The participants were not identifiable by name or school of attendance. The interventionist was the only person who knew the name of the students and which school they attended. As a normal course of action, the district made the results of the DRA2 and Dolch Sight-Word List results available to parents or guardians.

# Summary

Using archival data, in this research study the researcher evaluated the effectiveness of the Success Program conducted during the 2010-2011 and 2011–2012 school years. This was a district-wide initiative designed to elevate the literacy of third-grade African-American students reading below grade level. The study included a total of 200 students. There were 100 students per year for two years, which included 50 students (program group) who took part in the Success Program the first year (2010–2011) and a second group (comparison group) of 50 students who did not participate in the first year of the Success Program. Data collected for the second year (2011–2012) included scores of 50 students (program group) who took part in the Success Program and a comparison group of 50 students who did not participate in the Success Program.

The criteria for participation in the Success Program was students in the program group who were in the third-grade and at least one full grade below the third-grade level in literacy as measured by the DRA2 and the Dolch Sight-Word List. All of the

participants were African-American. The comparison
group was 50 African-American third-grade students
from the 2010-2011 school year and 50 students from
the 2011-2012 school year. The criteria for the
comparison group eligibility meant reading at one full
grade level below the third-grade literacy level per the
DRA and the Dolch Sight-Word List, but did not
participate in the Success Program. Therefore, for
the school year 2010-2011 the sample was composed
of 50 students in the program group and 50 students
in the comparison group.

For the school year 2010-2011 the sample
was composed of 50 students in the program group
and 50 students in the comparison group. Archived
pre- and post-tests from the DRA2 and Dolch Sight-
Word List had been recorded and were available for
both school years.

This study used a non-probability criterion
sampling method. The data in this study were
analyzed using the SPSS software program, Version
14.0 for Windows, MANOVA. Precautions were taken
for the protection of participants' rights by the original
data collectors. Chapter 4 reported the results of the
study including any changes or discrepancies to the

design or data collection processes. The baseline descriptive and demographics of the sample were discussed.

# Chapter 4: Analysis and Findings

## Introduction

Chapter 4 contained a reiteration of the hypotheses associated with this study as well as the data collection plan presented in Chapter 3. Because the results are concluded from archival data, there were no changes to instruments or strategies. How the data were collected was clarified. The results were presented through descriptive statistics and MANCOVA. The chapter concluded with a summary of the results.

Using archival data, the researcher evaluated the effectiveness of the Success Program, a district-wide initiative designed to elevate the literacy of third-grade, African-American students who were reading below grade level. The purpose of this study was to determine if the students who participated in the Success Program (program group) had significantly higher performance on four measures of achievement

– reading comprehension, oral reading fluency, instructional reading level, and sight word vocabulary – than children at a similar reading level who did not participate (comparison group) in the Success Program.

The hypotheses associated with each of the achievement scales were as follows:

## Hypothesis 1

H0: There is no statistically significant difference in reading comprehension between students who participated in the Success Program and students who did not participate in the Success Program, as reported by the DRA pre- and post-test assessment tool.

Ha: Students who participated in the Success Program are expected to achieve a statistically significant higher score in reading comprehension performance than students who did not participate in the Success Program, as reported by the DRA pre- and post-test assessment tool.

## Hypothesis 2

H0: There is no statistically significant difference in reading fluency between students who participated in the Success Program and students who did not participate in the Success Program, as reported by the DRA pre- and post-test assessment tool.

Ha: Students who participated in the Success Program are expected to achieve a statistically significant higher score in reading fluency performance than students who did not participate in the Success Program, as reported by the DRA pre- and post-test assessment tool.

## Hypothesis 3

H0: There is no statistically significant difference in instructional reading performance between students who participated in the Success Program and students who did not participate in the Success Program, as reported by the DRA pre- and post-test assessment tool.

Ha: Students who participated in the Success Program are expected to achieve a statistically significant higher score in instructional reading performance than students who did not participate in the Success Program, as reported by the DRA pre- and post-test assessment tool.

**Hypothesis 4**

H0: There is no statistically significant difference in sight-word recognition between students who participated in the Success Program and students who did not participate in the Success Program, as reported by the Dolch Sight-Word List pre- and post-test assessment tool.

Ha: Students who participated in the Success Program are expected to achieve a statistically significant higher score in sight-word recognition than students who did not participate in the Success Program, as reported by the Dolch Sight-Word List pre- and post-test assessment tool.

## Data Collection

The Success Program participants were located at all 10 elementary schools in the district. The Success Program was conducted in the same manner both years. In the beginning of each school year, the DRA2 and the Dolch Sight-Word List were administered in the third-grade classrooms as pre-tests. This test administration took place no later than the second week of October. For students to be considered eligible to participate in the Success Program they had to meet the following criteria: (a) African-American, (b) in the third-grade during participation in the program, (c) in a general education classroom, and (d) at least one grade level below in literacy according to four measures: reading fluency, reading comprehension, instructional reading performance, and sight-word recognition. The comparison group was composed of students who met the criteria to participate in the Success Program, but who did not participate.

Classroom teachers were asked to submit the names of students meeting the eligibility guidelines to the interventionist. The interventionist selected students from the classroom teacher recommendations for participation in the Success Program. There were 50 spaces for participation in the Success Program. Eligible students who were not placed in the Success Program due to limited space were placed in the comparison group. Parents were notified their child was receiving supplemental intervention during classroom literacy instruction. Parental consent was not required for participation in the Success Program.

The DRA2 and the Dolch Sight-Word List were administered no later than the second week of June to all third-grade students as post-tests. There were pre- and post-test scores available on all of the third-grade students for the school years 2010-2011 and 2011–2012. The test results were placed in each student's permanent record. The interventionist who oversaw the Success Program also had a copy of the DRA and Dolch Sight-Word List test results for all students. Archival data were collected to obtain the pre- and post-test scores for the program group students and the comparison group students.

The district's procedure to access this archival data was to request permission from the superintendent of schools, as well as the person

directly responsible for the security of the scores (see

Appendix A for the letter of cooperation). To ensure

confidentiality, the students were not identified by

name or by the school of enrollment. All students'

data were coded before their test results were

released to me.

## Results

Data were collected for 200 participants.

Data were assessed for univariate and multivariate

outliers. Univariate outliers were looked for by

creating standardized z scores for the following

scores at pretest and posttest: reading fluency,

reading comprehension, instructional reading, and

sight work recognition. Values greater than 3.29

standard deviations from the mean were considered

outliers; nine cases were removed as outliers. Eight

cases were removed from the treatment group and

one from the control group. All nine cases were

removed from the 2010-2011 school year. Of the

univariate outliers removed, six were removed

because of scores at pre-test and only three were

removed because of scores at post-test. Of the cases removed because of post-test scores, all scores were outliers because they were extremely low, as opposed to extremely high. Data were also assessed for multivariate outliers using Mahalanobis distances. The critical value was set at $\chi 2(10) = 29.59$, p = .001 (Tabachnick & Fidell, 2013). Four multivariate outliers were found and removed from the dataset. All four of those outliers were from the treatment group. Three of the outliers were from year 2010-2011 and one was from 2011-2012. Final data analysis was conducted on 187 participants.

## Descriptive Statistics

Of the 187 students, 88 (47%) were from school year 2010-2011 and 99 (53%) were from school year 2011–2012. Frequencies and percentages are presented in Table 1.

Table 1 - Frequencies and Percentages for Participation and School Year (N = 187)

| | 2011 | | 2012 | |
|---|---|---|---|---|
| Characteristic | N | % | N | % |
| Success Program | | | | |

|                    | 2011 |    | 2012 |    |
|--------------------|------|----|------|----|
| Characteristic     | N    | %  | N    | %  |
| Participated       | 39   | 44 | 49   | 50 |
| Did not participate| 49   | 56 | 50   | 50 |

Means, standard deviations, minimum, maximum, skew, and kurtosis were conducted on the entire sample (N = 187) for reading comprehension, reading fluency, instructional reading, and sight-word recognition at pretest and posttest. Means and standard deviations are presented in Table 2. Skew, kurtosis, minimum, and maximum are presented in Table 3.

Table 2 - Means and Standard Deviations for Reading Assessment Scores at Pre- and post-test (N = 187)

| Assessment | Pretest | | Post test | |
|---|---|---|---|---|
|  | M | SD | M | SD |
| Reading comprehension | 6.12 | 0.36 | 14.24 | 3.10 |
| Reading fluency | 4.17 | 0.44 | 9.55 | 1.71 |
| Instructional reading | 23.27 | 2.04 | 36.76 | 2.16 |
| Sight-word recognition | 12.65 | 6.02 | 39.06 | 3.75 |

*Table 3 - Min, Max, Skew and Kurtosis for Reading
Assessment Scores at Pre- and post-test (N = 187)*

| Assess- ment | Pretest | | | | Post test | | | |
|---|---|---|---|---|---|---|---|---|
| | Skew | Kurtosis | Min | Max | Skew | Kurtosis | Min | Max |
| Reading compre- hension | 2.99 | 8.82 | 6 | 8 | -0.94 | -0.12 | 7 | 19 |
| Reading fluency | 2.72 | 6.94 | 4 | 6 | 0.31 | -0.27 | 6 | 15 |
| Instruc- tional reading | -0.82 | 0.27 | 18 | 26 | -0.14 | -0.70 | 32 | 42 |
| Sight-word recognition | 0.21 | -0.76 | 0 | 29 | -1.83 | 3.23 | 23 | 49 |

## Assumption Testing

Prior to the analyses, data were assessed for normality using Shapiro-Wilk tests. The Shapiro-Wilk test is appropriate for sample sizes of up to 5,000 cases (Royston, 1995). Data did not meet the assumption of normality; however, with univariate F and large samples the central-limit thermo suggested distribution of the mean approached normality (Tabachnick & Fidell, 2013). Further, the F statistic was robust to violations of normality when they are not attributed to outliers (Tabachnick & Fidell, 2013). The results of the Shapiro-Wilk tests were presented in Table 4.

*Table 4 - Shapiro-Wilk Tests to Assess Normality*

| Variable | Statistic | p |
|---|---|---|
| Reading comprehension posttest | .94 | .001 |
| Reading fluency post-test | .88 | .001 |
| Instructional reading post-test | .88 | .001 |
| Sight-word recognition post-test | .65 | .001 |

Homogeneity of variance was assessed with four Levene's tests and was significant for reading comprehension, instructional reading, and sight-word recognition. Due to the violation of this assumption, the assumption of homogeneity of variance was found to be significant; however, ANOVAs were robust to this assumption as long as the cell sizes are relatively similar (largest: smallest = 1.5). The largest differences among the cells were 39:50, indicating similar cell sizes (Pallant, 2010). The results of the Levene's test were presented in Table 5.

*Table 5 - Levene's Tests to Assess Homogeneity of*

*Variance*

| Variable | Statistic | P |
|---|---|---|
| Reading comprehension posttest | 25.13 | .001 |
| Reading fluency posttest | 1.95 | .124 |
| Instructional reading posttest | 4.06 | .008 |
| Sight-word recognition posttest | 24.69 | .001 |

Homogeneity of covariance was assessed with Box's M and was found to be significant, $F = 7.69$, $p < .001$. The assumption was overly sensitive and was assessed at the .001 level. With similar sample sizes, a violation of the assumption was ignored (Tabachnick & Fidell, 2013). Absence of multicollinearity was assessed among the dependent variables to be certain they were not too related (Table 6). It was also assessed for the covariates (Table 7). The assumption was assessed using two Spearman ρ correlation matrices. The correlation coefficients were all < .90, indicating the assumption was met (Pallant, 2010).

*Table 6 - Spearman Correlations among Reading
Assessment Scores at Post-test*

| Variable | Reading fluency | Reading comprehension | Instructional reading |
|---|---|---|---|
| Reading comprehension | .79** | | |
| Instructional reading | .72** | .67** | |
| Sight-word recognition | .35** | .41** | .60** |

*Note.* **p < .01.

*Table 7 - Spearman Correlations among Reading
Assessment Scores at Pre-test*

| Variable | Reading fluency | Reading comprehension | Instructional reading |
|---|---|---|---|
| Reading comprehension | .37** | | |
| Instructional reading | .11 | .15 | |
| Sight-word recognition | .01 | .02 | .26** |

*Note.* **p < .01, *p < .05.

Pre- and post-test scores were correlated
using Spearman ρ correlations to determine if they

were related.  The correlations were found to be significant, indicating pre- and post-test scores were related.  Because of the relationship between pre- and post-test scores, pre-test scores were used as covariates in the MANCOVA analysis.  Results of the correlations between pre- and post-test scores were presented in Table 8.

*Table 8 - Spearman ρ Correlations between Pre- and post-test Scores*

| Variable | Reading comprehension posttest | Fluency post-test | Instructional reading posttest | Sight-word recognition post-test |
|---|---|---|---|---|
| Reading comprehension pretest | .06 | .12 | .08 | -.05 |
| Fluency pretest | .19* | .18* | .13 | .05 |
| Instructional reading pretest | .26** | .39** | .42** | .11 |
| Sight-word recognition pretest | .39** | .37** | .44** | .30** |

To assess Research Hypotheses 1-4 and to
determine if there were differences in reading
assessment scores post-test by group and school
year after controlling for reading assessment pretest
scores, a two-between MANCOVA was conducted.
The reading comprehension, reading fluency,
instructional reading, and sight-word recognition pretest scores were entered as covariates. The
dependent variables in the model were reading
comprehension, reading fluency, instructional reading,
and sight-word recognition post-test scores. The two-
between indicated there were two between level
independent variable measures. They were group
(treatment and control) and school year (2010-2011
and 2011–2012).

The main effect of group was significant, $F(4, 176) = 113.32$, $p < .001$, partial $\eta2 = 0.72$, indicating
there were differences on reading assessment scores
by whether or not the students participated in the
Success Program, after controlling for pretest scores
(Table 9). Examination of the individual ANCOVAs
demonstrated significant differences on reading
comprehension, reading fluency, and instructional

reading by group. The ANCOVA for reading comprehension was significant, $F(1, 179) = 189.05$, p $< .001$, partial $\eta 2 = 0.52$, indicating large differences between the two groups (Table 9). Those students who participated in the Success Program had a significantly higher mean reading comprehension scores (M = 16.39, SD = 1.32) than those students who did not participate (M = 12.33, SD = 2.98; Table 10). The ANCOVA for reading fluency was significant, $F(1, 179) = 331.86$, p $< .001$, partial $\eta 2 = 0.65$, indicating large differences between the two groups (Table 9). Those students who participated in the Success Program had a significantly higher mean reading fluency scores (M = 11.01, SD = 1.10) than those students who did not participate (M = 8.24, SD = 0.93; Table 10). The ANCOVA for instructional reading was significant, $F(1, 179) = 41.48$, p $< .001$, partial $\eta 2 = 0.19$, indicating small differences between the two groups (Table 9). Those students who participated in the Success Program had significantly higher mean instructional reading scores (M = 37.93, SD =1.81) than those students who did not participate (M = 35.72, SD = 1.92; Table 10). There were no differences on sight-word recognition post-test scores by group

The main effect of school year was significant, $F(4, 176) = 15.76$, $p < .001$, partial $\eta2 = 0.26$, indicating medium differences on the reading assessment scores by school year (2011 vs. 2012; Table 9). Examination of the individual ANCOVAs demonstrated significant differences on reading comprehension, instructional reading, and sight-word recognition by school year. The ANCOVA for reading comprehension was significant, $F(1, 179) = 62.36$, $p < .001$, partial $\eta2 = 0.26$, indicating medium differences on reading comprehension scores by school year, after controlling for pretest scores (Table 9). The students in the 2012 school year scored significantly higher on reading comprehension (M = 15.47, SD = 1.73) than those in the 2011 school year (M = 12.85, SD = 3.67; Table 10). The ANCOVA for instructional reading was significant, $F(1, 179) = 9.28$, $p = .003$, partial $\eta2 = 0.05$, indicating small differences on instructional reading scores by school year (Table 9). The students in the 2012 school year scored significantly higher on instructional reading (M = 37.23, SD = 2.15) than those in the 2011 school year (M = 36.23, SD =2.07; Table 10). The ANCOVA for sight-word recognition was significant, $F(1, 179) =$ 7.98, $p = .005$, partial $\eta2 = 0.04$, indicating small differences on sight-word recognition scores by school year (Table 9). The students in the 2012 school year scored significantly higher on sight-word recognition ($M = 40.08$, $SD = 2.67$) than those students in the 2011 school year ($M = 37.92$, $SD = 4.42$; Table 10). There were no significant differences in reading fluency post-test scores by the end of the school year.

The interaction term of group*school year was significant, $F(4, 176) = 12.08$, $p < .001$, partial $\eta2 = 0.22$, indicating small differences in the mean scores by the interaction effect, after controlling for pretest scores (Table 9). ANCOVAs and pairwise comparisons were assessed to determine where those differences lie. There were differences on reading comprehension, reading fluency, and sight-word recognition by the interaction term.

The ANCOVA conducted to assess reading comprehension was significant, $F(1, 179) = 39.92$, $p < .001$, partial $\eta2 = 0.18$, indicating there were small difference in reading comprehension by the interaction term (Table 9). Pairwise comparisons show that for the 2011 school year, students who participated in the Success Program (M = 16.10, SD = 1.60) had significantly higher mean reading comprehension scores than those who did not (M = 10.27, SD = 2.65; Table 10). And for the year 2012, students who participated in the Success Program (M = 16.61, SD = 1.04) had significantly higher mean reading comprehension scores than those students who did not participate (M = 14.36, SD = 1.55; Table 10). Additionally, non-participant students scored statistically lower in the year 2011 (M = 10.27, SD =2.65) than they did in 2012 (M = 14.36, SD =1.55; Table 10). The MANCOVA results were presented in Table 9. Figure 1 visually displayed the reading comprehension post-test scores by group and school year.

## Table 9 - MANCOVA for Reading Comprehension Scores by Intervention Participation and School Year

| Variable | MANOVA $F_{(4, 176)}$ | ANCOVA $F_{(1, 176)}$ | | | |
|---|---|---|---|---|---|
| | | Reading comprehension | Reading fluency | Instructional reading | Sight-word recognition |
| Group | 113.32** | 189.05** | 331.86** | 41.48** | 4.57 |
| Year | 15.76** | 62.36** | 1.85 | 9.28** | 7.98** |
| Group *Year | 12.08** | 39.92** | 11.50** | 1.74 | 8.94** |

Note. **$p < .01$.

## Table 10 - Means and Standard Deviations for Reading Comprehension Scores by Intervention Participation and School Year

| | 2010–2011 | | | | 2011–2012 | | | |
|---|---|---|---|---|---|---|---|---|
| | Participant | | Non-participant | | Participant | | Non-participant | |
| Test | M | SD | M | SD | M | SD | M | SD |
| Reading comprehension | 16.10 | 1.57 | 10.27 | 2.65 | 16.61 | 1.04 | 14.36 | 1.55 |
| Reading fluency | 11.15 | 1.29 | 7.94 | 0.85 | 10.90 | 0.92 | 8.54 | 0.91 |
| Instructional reading | 37.54 | 1.55 | 35.18 | 1.82 | 38.24 | 1.94 | 26.27 | 1.88 |
| Sight word recognition | 39.62 | 2.23 | 36.57 | 5.22 | 40.33 | 2.94 | 39.84 | 2.38 |

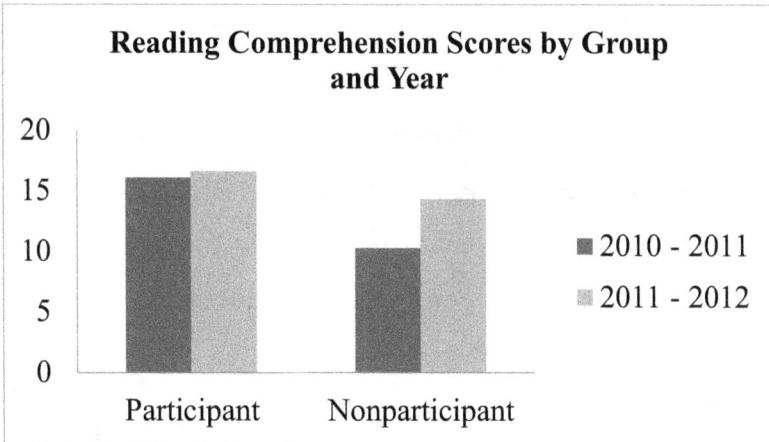

Figure 1. Bar chart of reading comprehension post-test scores by group and school year.

The benchmark for oral reading fluency in the Success Program was 11. The ANCOVA conducted to assess reading fluency was significant, $F(1, 179) = 11.50$, $p = .001$, partial $\eta 2 = 0.06$, indicating there were small difference in reading fluency by the interaction term (Table 10). Pairwise comparisons showed for the 2011 school year, students who participated in the Success Program ($M = 11.15$, $SD = 1.29$) had significantly higher mean reading fluency scores than those who did not ($M = 7.94$, $SD = 0.85$ Table 10). For the year 2012, students who participated in the Success Program ($M = 10.90$, $SD =$

0.92) had significantly higher mean reading fluency scores than those who did not participate (M = 8.54, SD =; 0.91 Table 10). Non-participants scored statistically lower in the year 2011 (M = 7.94, SD = 0.85) that they did in 2012 (M = 8.54, SD = 0.91; Table 10). Figure 2 visually displayed the reading fluency post-test scores by group and school year.

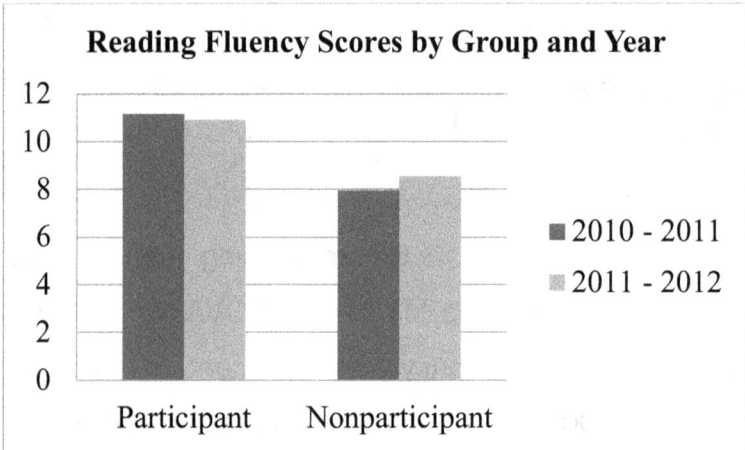

**Reading Fluency Scores by Group and Year**

*Figure 2. Bar chart of reading fluency post-test scores by group and school year.*

There were no differences in instructional reading post-test scores for the interaction term. Figure 3 displayed the instructional reading post-test scores by group and school year.

**Instructional Reading Scores by Group and Year**

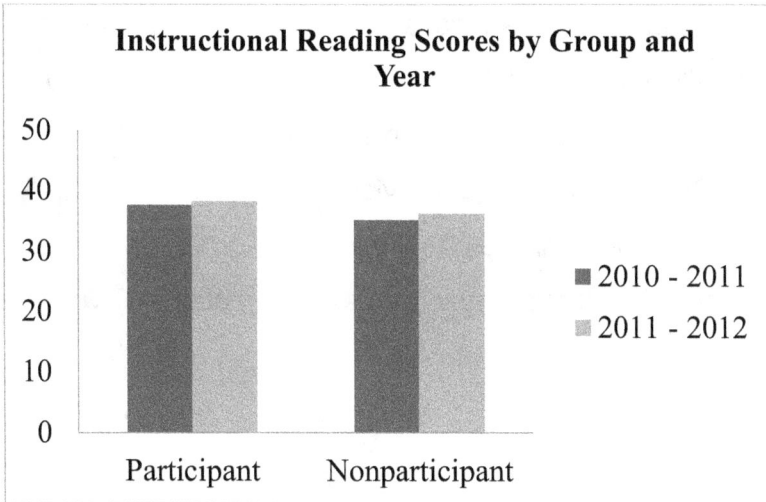

*Figure 3. Bar chart of instructional reading post-test scores by group and school year.*

The ANCOVA conducted to assess sight-word recognition was significant, $F(1, 179) = 8.94$, $p = .003$, partial $\eta2 = 0.05$, indicating there were small differences in sight-word recognition by the interaction term (Table 9). Pairwise comparisons showed for the 2011 school year, students who participated in the Success Program (M = 39.62, SD = 2.23) had significantly higher mean sight-word recognition scores than those who did not (M = 36.57, SD = 5.22; Table 10). There were no differences found in the year 2012 for students who participated or did not participate in the success program. Non-participants scored statistically lower in the year 2011 (M = 36.57, SD = 5.22) than they did in 2012(M = 39.84, SD = 2.39; Table 10). Figure 4 visually displayed the sight-word recognition post-test scores by group and school year. All null hypotheses must be rejected in favor of the alternative hypotheses.

**Sight Word Recognition Scores by Group and Year**

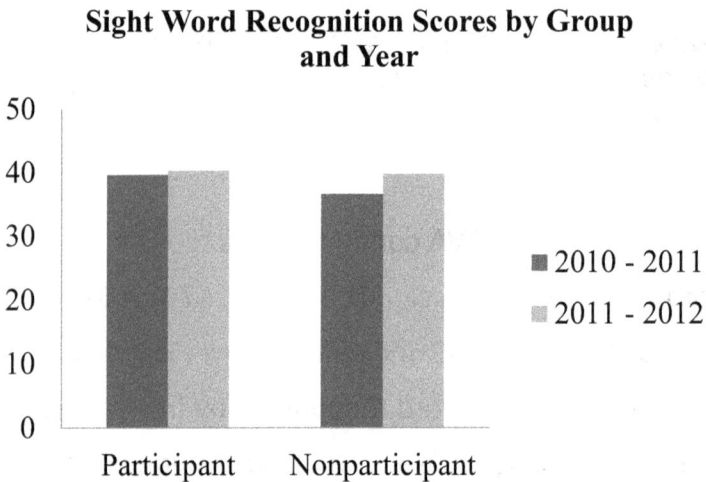

*Figure 4. Bar chart of sight-word recognition post-test scores by group and school year.*

## Summary

In summary, all null hypotheses were rejected in favor of the alternative hypotheses. To determine if there were differences in reading assessment scores post-test by group and school year after controlling for reading assessment pretest scores, a MANCOVA was conducted. The main effect for group and school year was found to be significant. The interaction effect of group and year was also found to be significant for reading comprehension, reading fluency, and sight-word recognition by the interaction of group and year. Pairwise comparisons were conducted to determine where those differences lie. For reading comprehension, reading fluency, and sight-word recognition there were similar outcomes. For each test, participants scored higher in 2011 and 2012 than non-participants. Additionally, non-participants scored higher in 2012 than 2011.

After a brief introduction, Chapter 5 proceeded with the findings of this study in an examination of the individual ANCOVAs for each research Hypothesis 1-4. Limitations of this study were scrutinized, followed by recommendations for future study. The implications for positive social change were explored, terminating with a conclusion of the study.

## Chapter 5: Discussion, Conclusions, and
## Recommendations

## Introduction

Literacy is the foundation for academic
success (Blanchett, 2009). If students cannot read,
they will most likely not be successful in school
(Hernandez, 2011). The State Supreme Court of New
Jersey in Abbott v. Burke (1981) ruled that inequality
in education existed in 31 school districts (Gewertz,
2005). The Abbott decision required the
implementation of a number of measures with
appropriate funding in the 31 districts deemed to have
special needs (Gomez, 2008). These districts are
considered the poorest in the state with large minority
populations that unable to afford to offer students an
adequate education (Gewertz, 2005). The State
Supreme Court found there was less expenditure per
pupil in these special needs' districts than the affluent
suburban districts in the state. The NJDOE was

ordered to offer an equal education by providing supplemental early literacy, health, and social services to these impoverished districts (Gewertz, 2005). The Success Program was implemented as a response to the NJDOE, citing the Sun Valley Lake school district for low student performance on literacy test scores of African-American students, particularly in the third grade.

This quantitative study adds to the literature addressing the low performance in early literacy as stated in the decision of the State Supreme Court of New Jersey ruling Abbott v. Burke (1981). The researcher investigated whether African-American, third-grade students who participated in the Success Program performed better on measures of academic achievement than students who did not participate in the program. The independent variable was the Success Program with two groups – students who participated in the program and students who did not. Academic achievement was the dependent variable, measured through reading comprehension, reading fluency, instructional reading performance, and sight-word recognition.

The participants were selected using a
nonprobability criterion sampling, which dictates a
quasi-experimental design that uses a pre- and post-
test method. The pretest was administered in the fall
of each year and the post-test was administered in
the spring of each year. The Success Program
included two assessment tools, the DRA and the
Dolch Sight-Word List, to assess students' literacy
skills. The interventionist who supervised the
program collected the data from the teachers.
Archival data on students in the Sun Valley Lake
School District participating in the Success Program
for the 2010-2011 and 2011-2012 school years were
used for these analyses. Using this approach,
reported conclusive statistics in response to the
research questions in this study.

## Interpretation of the Findings

There is a positive, congruent relationship
between the statistical findings and the theoretical
and conceptual framework presented in Chapter 2 of
this dissertation. Following is an overview of data
collected for each research question. The discussion

of each question is supported with research from the literature review, what was discovered, and what was surprising. As visual confirmation, bar charts have been added to each research question for clarification.

## Hypothesis 1

H01: There is no statistically significant difference in reading comprehension between students who participated in the Success Program and students who did not participate in the Success Program, as reported by the DRA pre- and post-test assessment tool.

Ha1: Students who participated in the Success Program are expected to achieve a statistically significant higher score in reading comprehension than students who did not participate in the Success Program, as reported by the DRA pre- and post-tests assessment tool.

Reading comprehension is affected by a person's previous knowledge and experience

(Rasinski et al., 2008). The No Child Left Behind act (NCLB; 2002) required third graders be measured in reading comprehension. The students in Sun Valley Lake have fallen short of literacy benchmarks for many years (NJDE, 2012b). The Success Program used Vygotsky's ZPD molding, scaffolding through planned opportunities for students to collaborate with their teacher and peers in a small group setting. Comprehension helps the reader to be able to act on, respond to, and transform the information presented in the written text in ways that demonstrate understanding (Rasinski et al., 2008).

To achieve the goals of increasing literacy, it is important to introduce emerging readers to vocabulary, language, and reading opportunities early in their lives. When assessing students' reading comprehension with the DRA, the goal for each student is to achieve a score in the independent range of at least 17. As Figure 1 demonstrates, students who participated in the Success Program during both years scored in the independent range. The researcher was expecting the students who did not participate in the program to score below the independent range. The researcher found

unexpected results in that students who did not
participate in year 2012 (M = 14.36), scored so
closely to those who participated in the Success
Program even without receiving the intervention (M =
16.61).

   After reflecting on what was different during
the two years in which the Success Program was
implemented, this researcher concluded the
difference was the infusion of small group instruction
into the classroom during the 2010-2011 school year.
The administration in school year 2010-2011 did not
require small group instruction and word walls to be
infused into the curriculum.  The administration in
school year 2011-2012 did require small group
instruction and word walls to be introduced into the
curriculum.  Therefore, every third-grade student was
placed into a small group.  Success Program
participants continued with the program and also
received small group instruction in their classroom.
All students in the classroom began participating in
groups of no more than five students reading at about
the same level.  There were 4-5 groups per class
dependent on the total number of students in the
class.  The group with the lowest literacy scores met

five days per week. The middle groups met four days per week. The group with the most advanced skills met three times per week. Each classroom teacher was given the opportunity to develop relationships during the small group experience that they were privy to during the first year of the Success Program. The difference in curriculum in the 2 school years may be the reason the students who did not participate in the Success Program during school year 2011-2012 scored similarly to those who did participate in the Success Program in school year 2011-2012.

## Hypothesis 2

H0: There is no statistically significant difference in reading fluency between students who participated in the Success Program and students who did not participate in the Success Program, as reported by the DRA pre- and post-test assessment tool.

Ha: Students who participated in the Success Program are expected to achieve a statistically significant higher score in reading fluency than

students who did not participate in the Success
Program, as reported by the DRA pre- and post-test
assessment tool.

In oral reading fluency the Success Program
participants were expected to meet the benchmark of
11. Oral reading fluency is a difficult skill to acquire
and involves quick and correct processing, which
entails automatic processing, the ability to smoothly
read large passages of text, and incidental or implicit,
learning (Duran, 2003). Grabe (2010) examined the
relationship between the amount of reading and high
achievement for fourth grade students. Grabe
concluded that reading, use of language, word
recognition, vocabulary, and fluent use of language
need to be reinforced. Grabe found a correlation
between the amount of reading, as well as
reinforcement of reading skills and the level of
academic achievement of fourth grade students.

Researchers (Hammer et al., 2010; Morgan &
Meier, 2008; Wasik & Hindman, 2011) suggested
poverty impacts language acquisition. Howard and
Coulge (2009) indicated children whose parents are
professionals have larger vocabularies than children
whose parents are receiving Temporary Assistance to

Needy Families (TANF). In terms of actual vocabulary by age 3, children whose parents are professionals had vocabularies of about 1,100 words and children whose parents that were TANF (social service) recipients had vocabularies of about 522 words (Howard & Coulge, 2009).

Sun Valley Lake Public School District is an economically-challenged urban district where 76.8% of the students are eligible for a free- or reduced-price lunch, which indicates they are living below the HUD poverty guidelines (Plainfield School District, 2011). Figure 2 illustrates participants in both years of the Success Program attained the benchmark of 11 in reading fluency. The students who participated in year 2010-2011 attained an average of 7.94, almost three points below the benchmark, whereas the students who did not participate in the Success Program during the 2011-2012 school year scored an average of 8.54, which is almost 2.5 points below the benchmark. However, the researcher was surprised that the 2011-2012 nonparticipants performed as well as they did. Scholars (Hammer et al., 2010; Morgan & Meier, 2008; Wasik & Hindman, 2011) have suggested students in Sun Valley Lake would not do well because of their SES and, therefore, the students vocabularies would be limited, impacting fluency as well as comprehension skills.

Oral reading fluency is one of the most difficult literacy skills to achieve. There was a significant difference between school years 2010-2011 or 2011-2012. The Success Program provided strategies to participants to increase their oral reading fluency during both school years. During the 2011-2012 school year, all third-grade students participated in small group instruction in class which emphasized oral reading fluency. Success Program participants met the benchmark of 11 in both school years. According to researchers (Hammer et al., 2010; Morgan & Meier, 2008; Wasik & Hindman, 2011) and the statistics from the 2010-2011 and 2011–2012 school years, the Success Program was positive in improving the oral reading fluency skills of the student participants in both years of the program. This segment of the study informs the 30 Abbott school districts in New Jersey with similar populations of an intervention that successfully increased oral reading fluency.

**Hypothesis 3**

H0: There is no statistically significant difference in instructional reading performance between students who participated in the Success Program and students who did not participate in the Success Program, as reported by the DRA pre- and post-test assessment tool.

Ha: Students who participated in the Success Program are expected to achieve statistically significant higher scores in instructional reading performance than students who did not participate in the Success Program, as reported by the DRA pre- and post-test assessment tool.

The benchmark for instructional reading performance in the Success Program was 38. Reading instructors need to ensure students are ready to properly establish the words of a text and then be able to extract the correct meaning (Conley et al., 2004). A student's instructional reading level can be assessed by word recognition and understanding of syntax (Troschitz, 2009). Third-grade students are expected to learn ways to decode multisyllabic words. Using the DRA, a third-grade student's instructional reading level is calculated by adding a student's score (from 26 the lowest to 38 the highest), which indicates the child's reading ability.

The benchmark of 38 was met at the highest scale for third-grade students who participated in the Success Program in school year 2010-2011 (M = 37.54). The benchmark was slightly exceeded for students who participated in the Success Program in school year 2011–2012 (M = 38.24). The students who did not participate in the Success Program did not meet the benchmark for third-grade students in school year 2010-2011 (M = 35.18). Students who did participate in the Success Program in school year 2011–2012 were just below the benchmark (M = 36.12). The researcher found unexpected results in - that students who did not participate in the Success Program came as close to the benchmark as the results indicated. The researcher did not expect these results because many students enter the Sun Valley Lake school district with limited exposure to early literacy experiences.

The researcher found students who participated in the Success Program were ready to enter the fourth grade understood syntax and had the ability to decode multi-syllabic words. The students who did not participate in the Success Program were not as prepared for the fourth grade in terms of expanded knowledge and critical thinking skills. As much as 50% of fourth grade curriculum (reading material) would be incomprehensible to students who are below grade level in reading (Schorr & Marchand, 2007). Schorr and Marchand (2007) found readers who are below proficient in third-grade remain so in high school.

**Hypothesis 4**

H0: There is no statistically significant difference in sight-word recognition between students who participated in the Success Program and students who did not participate in the Success Program, as reported by the Dolch Sight-Word List pre- and post-test assessment tool.

Ha: Students who participated in the Success
Program are expected to achieve a statistically
significant higher score in sight-word recognition than
students who did not participate in the Success
Program, as reported by the Dolch Sight-Word List
pre- and post-test assessment tool.

The Success Program used the benchmark
score of 41 in sight-word recognition. For the 2011
school year, students who participated in the Success
Program (M = 39.62) had significantly higher mean
sight-word recognition scores than those who did not
(M = 36.57). There were no differences found in the
year 2012 for students who participated or did not
participate in the success program.

Word recognition was an essential part of
reading comprehension because it included all
processes necessary to give a word a meaning and
its context (Troschitz, 2009). Troschitz defined sight-
word recognition as a discrete, observable response
controlled by a printed stimulus. Sight words were
recognized without mediation or phonetic analysis,
could be read from memory, and included not only
high frequency words, but any words that could be

read from memory (Meadan et al., 2008). By
mastering all of the Dolch sight words, a learner
would have been able to read at a third-grade level
(Meadan et al., 2008). Realizing over half of all third-
grade students in Sun Valley Lake were not proficient
in literacy, the Success Program (2010-2011 and
2011-2012?) implemented the Dolch Sight-Word List
as part of the literacy strategy plan.

The results of this segment of the study were
surprising. The ANCOVA for sight-word recognition
was significant, indicating small differences on sight-
word recognition scores by school year as well as by
group. The students who did not participate in
Success Program in the 2011–2012 school year (M =
39.84) scored visually higher on sight-word
recognition than students who participated in the
Success Program in the 2010-2011 school year (M =
39.62). In the school year 2011–2012, students
without intervention almost attained the exact level as
the students who participated in the Success
Program. The only evident change in the two school
years or the classroom was the administration and
what was being required in the classrooms. The
administration in school year 2011-2012 required

classroom teachers to provide small group instruction every day. Also, word walls were required in every subject area. Immersing students with word walls in the classroom was significant. The word walls in the classroom assist students in committing the words to memory. Committing more words to memory increases the ability to read more fluently (Duran, 2003). In the comparisons for the 2010-2011 school year, the researcher found students who participated in the Success Program had significantly higher mean sight-word recognition scores than those who did not. There were no differences found in the year 2011-2012 for students who participated or did not participate in the success program. Students in the 2010-2011 school year who participated in the Success Program met the third-grade benchmark of 41 in sight-word recognition. Those students who did not participate in the Success Program in the 2011–2012 school year benefited from the classroom small group instruction and word wall as evidenced by the results in Figure 4.

To summarize, research strongly supports early identification and intervention strategies to support students struggling with literacy skills. This quantitative study determined through archival data from the 2010-2011 and 2011-2012 school years that students who participated in the Success Program performed better on oral reading fluency, reading comprehension, instructional reading level, and sight-word recognition than students who did not participate in the Success Program.

There have been studies published on several of the larger Abbott school districts, but no published study has been documented with regard to approaches that may increase literacy of third-grade African-American students in Sun Lake Valley. This study has contributed significantly to the field of psychology because it has filled a knowledge gap that has existed since 1981 when the State Supreme Court of New Jersey issued the Abbott v. Burke ruling that African-American children were not receiving adequate education in 31 school districts.

## Summary of the Key Findings

All null hypotheses were rejected in favor of the alternative hypotheses. The overarching research question, "Is the Success Program a viable intervention to increase literacy skills of third-grade African-American students?" has been answered via the rejection of Research Hypotheses 1-4. Statistical analyses were conducted with results indicating there is conclusive empirical evidence of significant differences in reading scores post-test by group and school year across all four dependent variables.

In the 2010-2011 school year, students who participated in the Success Program had significantly higher mean reading comprehension scores than those who did not. And for the year 2011-2012, students who participated in the Success Program had significantly higher mean reading comprehension scores than those who did not participate. Non-participants scored statistically lower in the year 2010-2011 than they did in 2011-2012.

In the 2010-2011 school year, students who participated in the Success Program had significantly higher mean reading fluency scores than those who did not. And for the year 2011-2012, students who participated in the Success Program had significantly higher mean reading fluency scores than those who did not participate. Non-participants scored statistically lower in the year 2010-2011 than nonparticipants did in 2012.

The instructional reading scores indicated small main effects of both group and school year. Students who participated in the Success Program had significantly higher mean instructional reading scores than those who did not participate. Students in the 2011-2012 school year had significantly higher mean instructional reading scores than those in the 2010-2011 school year.

In the 2010-2011 school year, students who participated in the Success Program had significantly higher mean sight-word recognition scores than those who did not. There were no differences found in school year 2011-2012 for students who participated or did not participate in the success program.

To summarize the results, the Success Program realized favorable outcomes across all four measures (reading comprehension, reading fluency, instructional reading, and sight-word recognition) during both years the study was conducted. The students who did not participate in the Success Program in the second year (2011–2012) achieved unexpected favorable outcomes across three of the measures; reading comprehension, reading fluency, instructional reading. During the second year (2011–2012) the students who did not participate in the Success Program achieved almost identical results as the students who did participate in the Success Program on the measure of sight-word recognition.

There were two major differences in the classroom the second year of the study, which may explain the favorable outcomes on the students who did not participate in the Success Program. During the second year of the study, the third-grade general education teachers were directed to incorporate small group instruction as well as sight word walls in all subject areas within their classrooms. This was a huge instructional change between the two years of the study. Perhaps increasing small group instruction and visually immersing students with word walls had a positive effect on the results of the second-year data in the Success Program.

There is a connecting thread between this study and previous studies of small group instruction and improved literacy skills as evidenced in theoretical underpinnings previously mentioned such as Vygotsky and the RTI model. When there is relationship building through modeling and encouragement, it is expected the student will realize independence as confidence is gained (Bacon, 2005). The RTI model supports academic achievement focusing on literacy in relatively short periods. Vygotsky's ZPD is centered on small group instruction just as Tier 2 of the RTI model. Both Vygotsky and RTI expect the instructor to build upon a student's current knowledge base in small increments. This method will foster confidence in students to apply concepts learned independently.

Scaffolding is a process in which the students are provided a temporary framework for learning by the teachers as they gain confidence as they master a particular area of skill (Yildirim, 2008). The ZPD is the safe small group environment where the teacher models the appropriate exchanges of responses for the students to implement, first in the small group, and eventually in the classroom (Korepanova & Saphronova, 2011). The expectation of small group instruction in the Success Program was to provide a safe environment for students to have the confidence to ask questions or read text that they may not in the larger class setting. Several researchers (Miller, 2011; Tyner, 2009; Wasik, 2008) found positive results using scaffolding and ZPD, a Vygotskian theoretical framework often used when improving literacy skills for emerging readers receiving individualized instruction in small groups. The results of the research data from this study indicate utilizing small group instruction and the three-tier approach was a viable intervention for the Success Program to follow.

The researcher chose the resiliency theory as the theoretical framework for this study. The landmark New Jersey Supreme Court case, Abbott v. Burke, established a lack of academic and social–emotional support for the state's 31 poorest districts. The New Jersey Supreme Court allocated funds to sustain early academic learning as a means of eradicating the effects of poverty. This ruling established there is a segment of students across New Jersey that is economically vulnerable. The Abbott legislative order found students' achievement in school severely affects their social and economic success as adults.

The structure and methods of resiliency theory (Morales, 2008; Morales & Trotman, 2004; Ungar & Lerner, 2008) supports the current study's identification of common threads in increasing the literacy achievement of at-risk African-American third-grade students. According to Morales and Trotman (2004), the resiliency model suggests the dynamics affecting at-risk students are protective factors, vulnerability areas, and compensatory strategies. Resiliency theory aligns with and supports the current study illuminating the national (NCLB) and local (Abbott v. Burke) protective factors affecting the participants of the Success Program. Even more directly protecting students in the Sun Valley Lake School District is the New Jersey Supreme Court decision Abbott v. Burke enacted to ensure the poorest at-risk students in New Jersey have the proper funding to support academic achievement.

The findings from this study are congruent with previous research studies regarding resiliency identified in Chapter 2. For example, according to Morales (2008), resilient students are able to do well in school while dealing with adverse situations such as severe poverty or learning deficiencies. In the current study susceptibility to vulnerability manifests itself as students reading one grade level below what is expected in third-grade and the effect poverty may have in this situation. Research (Kim et al., 2010) on empirically supported intervention programs has revealed that intervening across multiple domains is more resourceful than focusing on just one aspect of a child's environment (Powers, 2010). Swanson et al. (2011) in their research on reading outcomes for at-risk early elementary students found skill development should not be concentrated in one specific area. They found positive results when skills were developed across several domains: vocabulary, letter recognition, comprehension, and oral reading fluency through 'read alouds' in small group instruction. The research conducted by Swanson et al. aligns well with Sun Valley Lake's supplemental reading program. The quantitative data results from the Success Program, which provided skill development as a collaborative intervention to African-American at-risk third-grade students during small group instruction in the areas of reading comprehension, oral reading fluency, instructional reading level, and sight-word recognition were found to have a significant impact on the students who participated in the program.

## Limitations of the Study

As with most studies there were several limitations to consider.  One study limitation was the sample participants were referred by classroom teachers, making the selection process not completely random and lending itself to possible bias. Another limitation was this study had no mechanism to evaluate any functioning deficits of the participants in terms of whether they lacked capacity or motivation to master the literacy skills in the Success Program. There was no indication whether any students participating in the study or those who did not participate received other assistance to raise their literacy skills.  With archival data there is no way to address these limitations.

The sample population was relatively small and limited to African-American students in the third-grade in the Sun Valley Lake school district, which makes it difficult to generalize to wider populations with the same environments (e.g. poverty, low literacy test scores).

## Recommendations

In terms of the importance of building relationships with low SES students in order to assist them with academic achievement, professional development for teachers is highly recommended. Ayalon (2007) proposed there are several programs that describe the utilization of educators or mentors for the academic progress of the students who belong to the lower SES and minority groups. It is observed that students at risk can be encouraged if they develop close relationships with the educators and mentors. Professional development is an essential part of training that helps educators realize the importance of relationship building when teaching students and elevating the students' skills.

In New Jersey, third-grade is the first-year students are tested to determine if they are meeting the NCLB benchmarks in literacy. It is recommended screenings start as soon as students enter the district so they may be placed in the Success Program or in small groups as needed to elevate their literacy skills. Sun Valley Lake school district would benefit working

with early childhood centers to provide stronger
literacy foundations for preschool students. This
recommendation to increase literacy skills in
preschoolers is supported by the New Jersey
Supreme Court Abbott v. Burke decision. Laosa
(2005) reported the foundation for strong literacy skills
is established before children reach age five.

Another recommendation is to conduct
research using participants instead of archival data.
The participants would be chosen through an
anonymous method. For example, just the children's
numbers on the DRAs would be used for
identification. This anonymity would eliminate the
possible bias of the classroom teacher. Perhaps it
would be beneficial if future studies included a short
survey to evaluate any functioning deficits of the
participants in terms of whether they lack capacity or
motivation to master the skills and whether any
students participating in the study received other
assistance to improve their literacy skills, such as an
outside tutoring service or parents reading nightly at
home.

Future research in terms of the relationship of
the students' assessments, such as the DRA and NJ-

ASK test results, may inform educators of areas for specific improvement.  Future studies could expand on and inform the existing body of knowledge by increasing information on topics such as demographics, including gender, ethnicity, and years in district, and whether the student receives free or reduced-price lunch, which would give researchers a broader base of data resources.  This kind of research would make the information gathered useful to other school districts with similar demographics in terms of which interventions were successful or not with comparable populations.

Another essential recommendation for future direction is the design of the curriculum of third-grade students.  Curriculum plays a vital role in the educational process.  A curriculum should be designed considering the views of a student, family and teacher. The backbone of curriculum should be laid with the interest(s), development levels, and personality of a student (Burns & Helman, 2009). The curriculum should be diverse, and the curriculum should consider the cultural, religious, and linguistic backgrounds of the students. The design of the curriculum should focus on methods and techniques to ensure that all materials are understandable by the students (McGrath et al., 2012). The learning environment of elementary school students requires a strong literacy curriculum including; effective teaching methods, daily planned schedules, assessments and daily tests admiring the student's goals (Larson, 2006). A curriculum includes social, physical and linguistic aspects, as these are the key learning areas. In addition to cultural diversity the instruction method should be designed under consideration of student's ability, interest and background (McGrath et al., 2012).

## Implications

### Positive Social Change

This research study has the potential to contribute significantly to positive social change by filling a significant gap in the literature. There have been studies published on several of the larger Abbott school districts, but no published study has documented approaches that may increase literacy of third-grade African-American students in Sun Lake

Valley. This study could contribute significantly to the field of educational psychology by filling a knowledge gap that has existed since 1981 when the State Supreme Court of New Jersey issued the Abbott v. Burke ruling that African-American children were not receiving adequate education in 31 school districts. Sun Valley Lake is one of the 31 special needs districts.

This research study sought to determine if the Success Program was an effective supplemental literacy intervention of third-grade African-American students who were at least one grade level below curriculum standards. The data indicates the Success Program realized favorable outcomes across all four measures (reading comprehension, reading fluency, instructional reading, and sight-word recognition) during both years the study was conducted. The favorable outcomes indicate the Success Program is an effective intervention. Even though the sample population was relatively small and limited to African-American students, it is probable the conclusions may be generalized to wider populations with the same environments (e.g. poverty, low literacy test scores). In New Jersey there are 30 additional Abbott school districts with very similar characteristics of the current study. This quantitative research study could be implemented even more widely if this study's conclusions are shown to be effective in other populations as well as in future research. Nationally, there are cities with significant populations with low literacy skills resulting in low test scores.

The connection between economic success and academic success means this research study could contribute to the economic success of American society's future citizens. Students not reading proficiently in third-grade are four times more likely to fail to achieve a high-school diploma (Hernandez, 2011). Lack of a high-school diploma may lessen a person's opportunities for financial stability. Lewis, Simon, Uzzell, Horwitz, and Casserly (2010) in a report for the Council of the Great City Schools noted that African-American males age 18 and over in 2008 represented only 5% of the total college student population but 36% of the total prison population. The Children's Defense Fund's (2012b) research found that two thirds of students who do not read at the proficient level by the end of fourth grade have a 75% chance of never attaining literacy proficiently and will most likely experience the incarceration and or the social service system. The Success Program is a positive intervention to improve the literacy skills of African-American students and has the potential to ultimately reduce the dropout rate of high school students, reduce occurrences with the justice and social service systems.

## Conclusion

Educational research, law, and policy point out that the quandary of African-American students not reading on grade level is persistent and pervasive. If interventions are not designed to address issues of inadequate allocation of educational resources, appropriate cultural curricula, and teacher preparation, the impact to society may have far reaching implications. There appear to be correlations between literacy, the penal system, and poverty. Poverty is pervasive in African-American families according to the Portrait of Inequality 2012 Black Children in America (Children's Defense Fund, 2012a). On average, African-American children arrive at kindergarten and/or first grade with lower levels of school readiness than White children (Farkas, 2003).

Literacy is an essential skill to function effectively in society. One of the significant components of education is learning to comprehend and know the meaning of text. It is vital for students to know the significance of what they are reading or the effort is pointless. As Ari (2011) noted, improved comprehension will increase the vocabulary of the learners, and they will gain confidence in writing and reading. Students will be able to read fluently mimicking their normal speech patterns (Ari, 2011).

The findings of this study add to the body of existing knowledge by reporting empirical research findings supporting, the three-tier approach of the Success Program which was based on the RTI model, largely because it has been proven effective (Greenwood et al., 2011; McGrath et al., 2012; Samuels, 2008; Vellutino et al., 2008) and can be used to improve literacy achievement in elementary schools. The RTI model framework aligned with the Success Program because both models use differentiating instructional strategies for students based on their demonstrated need. RTI is a method that uses measurement starting with a universal screening of the students (McGrath et al., 2012).

The results of this study may be beneficial for gaining a deeper understanding of an intervention program that raised literacy skills in third-grade African-American who were one grade level below the benchmark assessment.  The results of this study are conclusive in that students were academically resilient.  The participants in the Success Program were able to engage in relationships with their supplemental teacher and subsequently increase their literacy.  Such significant gains in literacy skills were realized with a 40-minute intervention twice per week, and these results demonstrate the Success Program is an effective intervention for improving children's literacy skills.

# References

Allen-Kyle, P., & Parello, N. (2001). Food for thought: Expanding school breakfast to *NJ students*. Retrieved from www.aecf.org/KnowledgeCenter/Publications.aspx?pubguid= %7B9B0AED35-F461-40F8-8EC1-C5DB426C2672%7D

Annie E. Casey Foundation. (2012). *Double jeopardy: How third-grade reading skills and poverty influence high school graduation*. Retrieved from http://www.aecf.org/~/media/Pubs/Topics/Education/Other/D oubleJeopardyHowThirdGradeReadingSkillsandPovery/Dou bleJeopardyReport030812forweb.pdf

Ainsworth, M. T., Ortlieb, E., Cheek, E. H., Pate-Simnacher, R, & Fetters, C. (2012). First-grade teachers' perception and implementation of a semi-scripted reading curriculum. *Language and Education, 26*, 77–90. doi:10.1080/09500782.2011.618540

American Psychological Association. (2010). *Publication manual of the American Psychological Association* (6th ed.). Washington, DC: Author.

Ari, O. (2011). Fluency interventions for developmental readers: Repeated readings and wide reading. *Research & Teaching in Developmental Education, 28*, 5–15. Retrieved from http://www.nyclsa.org/index.html#

Atkinson, G., Dietz, S., & Neumayer, E. (2007). *Handbook of sustainable development*. Albany, NY: Edward Elgar Publishing.

Ayalon, A. (2007). A model for teacher mentoring of poor and minority children: A case study of an urban Israeli school mentoring program. *Mentoring & Tutoring: Partnership in Learning, 15*, 5–23. doi:10.1080/13611260601037348

Bacon, S. (2005). Reading coaches: Adapting an intervention model for upper elementary and middle school readers. *Journal of Adolescent & Adult Literacy, 48*(5), 416–427. doi:10.1598/JAAL.48.5.5

Beaver, J. M. (2006). *Teacher guide: Developmental Reading Assessment, Grades K–3* (2nd ed.). Parsippany, NJ:

Pearson Education.

Berk, L. E. (2007). *Child development* (7th ed.). Noida, India: Dorling Kindersley.

Benard, B. (2004). *Resiliency: What we have learned*, San Francisco, CA: WestEd.

Bhattacharya, J., Currie, J., & Haider, S. (2006). Breakfast of champions? The school breakfast program and the nutrition of children and families. *Journal of Human Resources 41*, 445–466. Retrieved from http://jhr.uwpress.org/

Blanchett, W. J. (2009). A retrospective examination of urban education: From Brown to the desegregation of African-Americans in special education—It is time to "go for broke." *Urban Education, 44*, 370–388. doi:10.1177/0042085909338688

Blanchett, W. J., Mumford, V., & Beachum, F. (2005). Urban school failure and disproportionality in a post-Brown era: Benign neglect of the constitutional rights of students of color. *Remedial and Special Education, 26*, 70–81. doi:10.1177/07419325050260020201

Burchinala, M., Vandergriftb, N., Piantac, R., & Mashburnc, A. (2010). Threshold analysis of association between child care quality and child outcomes for low-income children in pre-kindergarten programs. *Early Childhood Research Quarterly, 25*, 166–176. doi:10.1016/j.ecresq.2009.10.004

Burns, M. K., & Helman, L. A. (2009). Relationship between language skills and acquisition rate of sight words among English language learners. *Literacy Research and Instruction, 48*, 221–232. doi:10.1080/19388070802291547

Champion, T., Hyter, Y., McCabe, A., & Bland-Stewart, L. (2003). A matter of vocabulary": Performances of low-income African-American Head Start children on the Peabody Picture Vocabulary Test-III. *Communication Disorders Quarterly, 24*, 121–127. doi:10.1177/15257401030240030301

Children's Defense Fund. (2004). Children and the long-term effects of poverty. Retrieved from www.childrensdefense.org

Children's Defense Fund. (2012a). *Portrait of inequality 2012— Black children in America*. Retrieved from http://www.childrensdefense.org/child-research-data-publications/data/portrait-of-inequality-2011.html

Children's Defense Fund. (2012b). *State of America's children 2012 handbook*. Retrieved from http://www.childrensdefense.org/child-research-data-publications/data/protect-children-not-guns-2012.html

Conley, C. M., Derby, K., Roberts-Gwinn, M., Weber, K. P., & McLaughlin, T. F. (2004). An analysis of initial acquisition and maintenance of sight words following picture matching and copy, cover, and compare teaching methods. *Journal of Applied Behavior Analysis, 37*, 339–349. doi:10.1901/jaba.2004.37-339 I stopped reviewing here.

Cullinan, D., & Kauffman, J. M. (2005). Do race of student and race of teacher influence ratings of emotional and behavioral problem characteristics of students with emotional disturbance? *Behavioral Disorders, 30*, 393–402. Retrieved from www.ccbd.net/behavioraldisorders/

Dee, T. S., & Jacob, B. (2011). The impact of No Child Left Behind on student achievement. *Journal of Policy Analysis & Management, 30*, 418–446. doi:10.1002/pam.20586

Dolch, E. W. (1942). *The Dolch basic sight word test*. Champaign IL: Garrard.

Downey, J. A. (2008). Recommendations for fostering educational resilience in the classroom. *Preventing School Failure, 53*, 52–64. doi:0.3200/PSFL.53.1.56-64

Dreher, M. J., & Zenge, S. D. (1990). Using metalinguistic awareness in first grade to predict reading achievement in third and fifth grades. *The Journal of Educational Research, 84*, 13–21. Retrieved from: http://www.tandfonline.com/loi/vjer20

Dunn, M., Cole, C., & Estrada, A. (2009). Referral criteria for special education: General education teachers' perspectives in Canada and the United States of America. *Rural Special Education Quarterly, 28*(1), 28–37. Retrieved from http://acres-sped.org/journal

Duran, E. (2003). *Systematic instruction in reading for Spanish-speaking students*. Springfield, IL: Charles C. Thomas Publishers.

Ebersole, J. L., & Kapp, S. A. (2007). Stemming the tide of overrepresentation: Ensuring accurate certification of African-American students in programs for the mentally retarded. *School Social Work Journal, 31*(2), 1–16. Retrieved from http://lyceumbooks.com/sswjournal.htm

Elias, A. T., & Torres, E. (2007). *Supplemental early literacy intervention for first grade English language* (Doctoral dissertation). Retrieved from ProQuest Dissertations and Theses database. (UMI No. 3295495)

Farkas, G. (2003). Cognitive skills and noncognitive traits and behaviors in stratification processes. *Annual Review of Sociology, 29,* 541–562. doi:10.1146/annurev.soc.29.010202.100023

Fernandez, N. (2009). *Early childhood education: The sustainability of the benefits of preschool participation in Abbott districts* (Doctoral dissertation). Retrieved from ProQuest Dissertations and Theses database. (UMI No. 3416599).

Fien, H., Santoro, L., Baker, S. K., Park, Y., Chard, D. J., Williams, S., & Haria, P. (2011). Enhancing teacher 'read alouds' with small-group vocabulary instruction for students with low vocabulary in first-grade classrooms. *School Psychology Review, 40,* 307–318. Retrieved from www.nasponline.org/publications/spr/

Gardner, R. I., & Miranda, A. H. (2001). Improving outcomes for urban African-American students. *Journal of Negro Education, 70,* 255–263. doi:10.2307/3211278

Gewertz, C. (2005). A level playing field. *Education Week, 24*(17), 40–48. Retrieved from http://www.edweek.org/

Gewertz, C. (2011). N. J. High court's funding decision leaves few satisfied. *Education Week, 30*(33), 18–23. Retrieved from http://www.edweek.org/

Gomez, J. C. (2008). Hope for children trapped in failing schools: The promise of "Crawford v. Davy." *Peabody Journal of Education, 83,* 297–321. doi:10.1080/01619560801997143

Grabe, W. (2010). Fluency in reading—Thirty-five years late. *Reading in a Foreign Language, 22,* 71–83. Retrieved from http://nflrc.hawaii.edu/rfl/

Gravetter, F., & Wallnau, L. (2007). *Statistics for the behavioral sciences.* Belmont, CA: Thomson Higher Education.

Greenwood, C. R., Bradfield, T., Kaminski, R., Linas, M., Carta, J. J., & Nylander, D. (2011). The response to intervention (RTI) approach in early childhood. *Focus on Exceptional Children, 43*(9), 1–22. Retrieved from http://www.lovepublishing.com/catalog/focus_on_exceptional_children_31.html

Gunn, B., Smolkowski, K., Biglan, A., & Black, C. (2002). Supplemental instruction in decoding skills for Hispanic and non-Hispanic students in early elementary school: A follow-up. *Journal of Special Education, 36*(2), 69–79. doi:10.1177/00224669020360020201

Hammer, C., Farkas, G., & Maczuga, S. (2010). The language and literacy development of Head Start children: A study using the family and child experiences survey database. *Language, Speech & Hearing Services in Schools, 41*(1), 70–83. doi:10.1044/0161-1461(2009/08-0050)

Harlow, C. W. (2003). *Education and correctional populations* (Special report NCJ 195670). Retrieved from www.bjs.gov/content/pub/pdf/ecp.pdf

Harry, B., & Anderson, M. G. (1995). The disproportionate placement of African-American males in special education programs: A critique of the process. *Journal of Negro Education, 63*, 602–619. doi:10.2307/2967298

Harry, B., Klingner, J. K., & Hart, J. (2005). African-American families under fire: Ethnographic views of family strengths. *Remedial and Special Education, 26*, 101–112. doi:10.1177/07419325050260020501

Hart, B., & Risley, T. (2003). The early catastrophe: The 30-million word gap by age 3 [Electronic version]. *American Educator, 27*(1), 4–9.

Hart, J. E., Cramer, E. D., Harry, B., Klingner, J. K., & Sturges, K. M. (2010). The continuum of "troubling" to "troubled" behavior: Exploratory case studies of African-American students in programs for emotional disturbance. *RASE: Remedial & Special Education, 31*(3), 148–162. doi:10.1177/0741932508327468

Henderson, N., & Milstein, M. M. (2003). *Resiliency in schools: Making it happen or students and educations* (Updated ed.). Thousand Oaks, CA: Corwin Press.

Hernandez, D. J. (2011). *Double jeopardy: How third 'grade reading skills and poverty influence high school graduation.* Baltimore, MD: Annie E. Casey Foundation. Retrieved from the Annie E. Casey Foundation website: www.aecf.org/KnowledgeCenter/Publications.aspx?pubguid= {8E2B6F93-75C6-4AA6-8C6E-CE88945980A9}

Hosterman, S. J., DuPaul, G. J., & Jitendra, A. K. (2008). Teacher ratings of ADHD symptoms in ethnic minority students: Bias or behavioral difference? *School Psychology Quarterly, 23*, 418–435. doi:10.1037/a0012668

Howard, T., Dresser, S. G., & Kunklee, D. R. (2009). *Poverty is not a learning disability: Equalizing opportunities for low SES.* New York, NY: Corvin Press.

Irving, M. A., & Hudley, C. (2005). Cultural mistrust, academic outcome expectations, and outcome values among African-American adolescent men. *Urban Education, 40*, 476–496. doi:10.1177/0042085905278019

Jones, L., & Menchetti, B. M. (2001). Identification of variables contributing to definitions of mild and moderate mental retardation in Florida. *Journal of Black Studies, 31*, 619–634. doi:10.1177/002193470103100506

Johnson, D. W., & Johnson, R. T. (1999). *Learning together and alone* (5th ed.). Needham Heights, MA: Allyn and Bacon.

Kearns, T., Ford, L., & Linney, J. A. (2005). African-American student representation in special education programs. *Journal of Negro Education, 74*, 297–310. doi:10.1007/978-0-387-71799-9_150

Kim, Y., Petscher, Y., Schatschneider, C., & Foorman, B. (2010). Does growth rate in oral reading fluency matter in predicting reading comprehension achievement? *Journal of Educational Psychology, 102*, 652–667. doi:10.1037/a0019643

Kleinspehn-Ammerlahn, A., Riediger, M., Schmiedek, F., Von Oertzen, T., Li, S.-C., & Lindenberger, U. (2011). Dyadic drumming across the lifespan reveals a zone of proximal development in children. *Developmental Psychology, 47*, 632–644. doi:10.1037/a0021818

Korepanova, I. A., & Saphronova, M. A. (2011). Three concepts reflecting the reality of child development: Ability to learn, zone of proximal development and scaffolding [English version]. *Cultural-Historical Psychology, 2011*(2), 74–83. Retrieved from http://psyjournals.ru/en/kip/

Kostewicz, D. E. (2012). Implementing systematic practice to build reading fluency via repeated readings. *New England Reading Association Journal, 47*(2), 17–22. Retrieved from http://www.nereading.org/

Kozulin, A. (2009). Review of "Vygotsky's legacy: A foundation for research and practice" and "Key to learning: The technology of child development—Vygotskian approach to early education." *Journal of Cognitive Education and Psychology, 8*, 216–221. Retrieved from www.springerpub.com/product/19458959

Kozulin, A. (2011). The dynamics of the schoolchild's mental development in relation to teaching and learning. *Journal of Cognitive Education & Psychology, 10*, 198–211. doi:10.1891/19458959.10.2.198

Larson, J. (2006). Multiple literacies, curriculum, and instruction in early childhood and elementary school. *Theory Into Practice, 45*, 319–329. doi:10.1207/s15430421tip4504_5

Laosa, L. M. (2005). *Effects of preschool on educational*

*achievement* (National Institute for Early Education Research Working Paper). Retrieved from http://nieer.org/resources/research/EffectsPreK.pdf

Lewis, S., Simon, C., Uzzell, R., Horwitz, A., & Casserly, M. (2010). *A call for change: The social and educational factors contributing to the outcomes of Black males in urban schools.* Retrieved from http://www.edweek.org/media/black_male_study.pdf

Luthar, S. S, Cicchetti. D., & Becker, B. (2000). The construct of resilience: A critical evaluation and guidelines for future work. *Child Development, 71*, 543–562. doi:10.1111/1467-8624.00164

Lo, Y., & Cartledge, G. (2006). FBA and BIP: Increasing the behavior adjustment of African-American boys in schools. *Behavioral Disorders, 31*(2), 147–161. Retrieved from https://www.cec.sped.org/

Markova M. V., & Medvedev A. M. (2010). Organization of zone of proximal development of planning cognitive function in schoolchildren. *Cultural-Historical Psychology, 2010*(1), 103–111. Retrieved from http://мгппу.рф/

McGrath, G. L., McLaughlin, T. F., Derby, K. M., & Bucknell, W. (2012). The effects of using reading racetracks for teaching of sight words to three third-grade students with learning disorders. *Educational Research Quarterly, 35*(3), 50–66. Retrieved from http://erquarterly.org/

Meadan, H., Stoner, J. B., & Parette, H. P. (2008). Sight-word recognition among young children at-risk: Picture-supported vs. word-only. *Assistive Technology Outcomes and Benefits, 5*, 45–58. Retrieved from http://www.atia.org/i4a/pages/index.cfm?pageid = 3305

Meece, J. (2010). *Handbook of research on schools, schooling and human development.* New York, NY: Taylor & Francis.

Mellard, D. E., & Johnson, E. (2008). *A practitioner's guide to implementing response to intervention.* Thousand Oaks, CA: Corwin Press.

Miller, P. H. (2010). *Theories of developmental psychology* (5th ed.). New York, NY: Worth.

Morales, E. E. (2008). Academic resilience in retrospect: Following up a decade later. *Journal of Hispanic Higher Education, 7*(3), 228–248. doi:10.1177/1538192708317119

Morales, E., & Trotman, F. (2004). *Promoting academic resilience in multicultural America: Factors affecting student success.* New York, NY: Peter Lang.

Morgan, P. L., & Meier, C. R. (2008). Dialogic reading's potential to improve children's emergent literacy skills and behavior. *Preventing School Failure, 52*(4), 11–16. doi:10.3200/PSFL.52.4.11-16

Mullen, C. A. (2007). Curriculum leadership development: A guide for aspiring school leaders. New York, NY: Routledge.

National Center for Educational Statistics, U.S. Department of Education. (2003). National assessment of adult literacy. Retrieved from http://nces.ed.gov/naal/

National Center for Educational Statistics, U.S. Department of Education. (2012). Retrieved from http://nces.ed.gov/ccd/districtsearch/district_detail.asp?Search=1&details=1&InstName=plainfield&State=34&Zip=07060&DistrictType=1&DistrictType=2&DistrictType=3&DistrictType=4&DistrictType=5&DistrictType=6&DistrictType=7&NumOfStudentsRange=more&NumOfSchoolsRange=more&ID2=3413140

National Reading Panel. (2000). *Teaching children to read: An evidence-based assessment of the scientific research literature on reading and its implications for reading instruction* (NIH Publication No. 00-4769). Washington, DC: U.S. Government Printing Office.

New Jersey Data Bank. (2012). *Education funding report.* A project of the School of Public Affairs and Administration, Rutgers University-Campus at Newark retrieved from http://njdatabank.newark.rutgers.edu

New Jersey Department of Education. (2011a). *Bureau of Justice Statistics special report: Education and correctional populations* (NCJ 195670). Retrieved from http://bjs.ojp.usdoj.gov/content/pub/ascii/ecp.txt

New Jersey Department of Education. (2011b). *New Jersey taxpayers guide.* Retrieved from www.state.uj.us/education/guide/2011/intro.pdf.

New Jersey Department of Education. (2011c). *New Jersey assessment of skills and knowledge (NJ ASK), grades 3, 4, and 5.* Spring 2011. Retrieved from http://www.state.nj.us/education/assessment/es/njask_info_guide.pdf

New Jersey Department of Education. (2012a). *New Jersey assessment of skills and knowledge (NJ ASK), grades 3, 4, and 5.* Spring 2012. Retrieved from http://www.state.nj.us/education/assessment/es/njask_info_guide.pdf

New Jersey Department of Education. (2012a change to b). *New Jersey historical report card data 1995–2012*. Retrieved from www.state.nj.us/education/reportcard/index.html

No Child Left Behind Act of 2001, Pub. L. No. 107–110, § 115, Stat. 1425. (2002).

Olmeda, R. E., & Kauffman, J. M. (2003). Socio-cultural considerations in social skills training research with African-American students with emotional or behavioral disorders. *Journal of Developmental and Physical Disabilities, 15*, 101–121. doi:10.1023/A:1022871232435

Pallant, J. (2010). *SPSS Survival Manual* (4th ed.). New York, NY: McGraw-Hill.

Paris, S. G., & Hoffman, J. V. (2004). Reading assessments in kindergarten through third grade: Findings from the Center for the Improvement of Early Reading Achievement. *Elementary School Journal, 105*, 199–217. doi:10.1086/428865

Pearson Education. (2009). *Developmental reading assessment technical manual* (2nd ed.). Upper Saddle River, NJ: Author.

Pilonieta, P. (2012). How fast is too fast? Fluency instruction in the classroom. *California Reader, 45*(3), 8–12. Retrieved from http://www.californiareads.org/display.asp?p=Home

Pizzo, J. S. (2008). *Barron's New Jersey Ask 7 language arts literacy test*. New York, NY: Barron's Educational Series.

Powers, J. D. (2010). Ecological risk and resilience perspective: A theoretical framework supporting evidence-based practice in schools. *Journal of Evidence-Based Social Work, 7*(5), 443–451. doi:10.1080/15433714.2010.509216

Rasinski, T., Brassell, D., & Yopp, H. (2008). *Comprehension that works: Taking students beyond ordinary understanding to deep comprehension*. New York, NY: Shell Education.

Ready, D. D. (2010). Socio-economic disadvantage, school attendance, and early cognitive development: The differential effects of school exposure. *Sociology of Education, 83*(4), 271–286

Risko, V. J., & Walker-Dalhouse, D. (2007). Tapping students' cultural funds of knowledge to address the achievement gap. *Reading Teacher, 61*, 98–100. doi:10.1598/RT.61.1.12

Ross, S. M., Potter, A., Paek, J., McKay, D., Sanders, W., & Ashton, J. (2008). Implementation and outcomes of supplemental educational services: The Tennessee state-wide evaluation study. *Journal of Education for Students Placed at Risk, 13*, 26–58. doi:10.1080/10824660701860391

Royston, P. (1995). Remark AS R94:A Remark on algorithm
AS181:The W-test for normality. *Journal of the Royal
Statistical Society, 44*, 547–551. Retrieved from
http://www.rss.org.uk/site/cms/contentCategoryView.asp?cat
egory=90

Samuels, C. A. (2008). "Response to intervention" sparks
interest, questions. *Education Digest, 73*(8), 21–24.
Retrieved from www.eddigest.com

Scammacca, N., Vaughn, S., Roberts, G., Wanzek, J., &
Torgesen, J. K. (2007). *Extensive reading interventions in
grades K–3: From research to practice.* Portsmouth, NH:
RMC Research Corporation, Center on Instruction.
Retrieved from www.centeroninstruction.org

Schorr, L. B., & Marchand, V. (2007). *Pathway to children ready
for school and succeeding at third grade.* Retrieved from
www.cssp.org/publications/pathways-to-outcomes/3rd-
grade-pathway-pdf9-07.pdf

Sirvani, H. (2007). The effect of teacher communication with
parents on students' mathematics achievement. *American
Secondary Education, 36*(1), 31–46. Retrieved from
www1.ashland.edu/coe/about-college/american-secondary-
education-journal

Slavin, G., Lake, C., Cheung, A., & Davis, S. (2008). *Beyond the
basics: Effective reading programs for the upper elementary
grades.* Retrieved from
http://www.bestevidence.org/word/upper_elem_read_sep_16
_2008.pdf

Snow, C. E. (2002). *Reading for understanding: Toward an R &
D program in reading comprehension. Monterey.* Santa
Monica, CA: RAND.

Snow, D. (2005). *Classroom strategies for helping at-risk
students.* New York, NY: ASCD.

Snow, C. E., Burns, M. S., & Griffin, P. (1998). *Preventing
reading difficulties in young children.* Washington, DC:
National Academy Press.

Swain, M., & Lapkin, S. (2000). Task-based second language
learning: The uses of the first language. *Language Teaching
Research, 4*, 251–274. doi:10.1177/136216880000400304

Swanson, E., Solis, M., Ciullo, S., & McKenna, J. W. (2012).
Teachers' perceptions and instructional practices in response
to intervention implementation. *Learning Disability Quarterly,
35*, 115–126 doi:10.1177/0731948711432510

Tabachnick, B. G., & Fidell, L. S. (2013). *Using multivariate statistics* (6th ed.). Boston, MA: Allyn and Bacon.

Teale, W. H., Paciga, K. A., & Hoffman, J. L. (2007). Beginning reading instruction in urban schools: The curriculum gap ensures a continuing achievement gap. *Reading Teacher, 61,* 344–348. doi:10.1598/RT.61.4.8

Troschitz, R (2009). *Testing reading comprehension: Problems and principles.* Munich, Germany: GRIN Verlag.

Turuk, M. (2008). The relevance and implications of Vygotsky's socio-cultural theory in the second language classroom. *Annual Review of Education, Communication & Language Sciences, 5,* 244–262. Retrieved from http://research.ncl.ac.uk/ARECLS/

Tyner, B. (2009). *Small-group reading instruction: A differentiated teaching model for beginning and struggling readers.* New York, NY: International Reading Association.

Ungar, M. (2010). What is resilience across cultures and contexts? Advances to the theory of positive development among individuals and families under stress. *Journal of Family Psychotherapy, 21*(1), 1–16. doi:10.1080/08975351003618494

Ungar, M., & Lerner, R. M. (2008). Introduction to a special issue of research in human development: Resilience and positive development across the life span: A view of the issues. *Research in Human Development, 5*(3), 135–138. doi:10.1080/15427600802273961

U.S. Census Bureau. (2010). Poverty in the United States. Retrieved from http://www.npc.umich.edu/poverty/

U.S. Census Bureau. (2012). *Statistical abstract of the United States: 2012.* Retrieved from http://www.census.gov/prod/2011pubs/12statab/educ.pdf

U.S. Department of Education. (2011). *ESEA waiver request from New Jersey.* Retrieved from www2.ed.gov/policy/eseaflex/approved-requests/nj.pdf

U. S. Department of Housing and Urban Development. (2012). *HUD's public housing program.* Retrieved from http://portal.hud.gov/hudportal/HUD?src=/topics/rental_assist ance/phprog

VanDerHeyden, A. M., Snyder, P. A., Broussard, C., & Ramsdell, K. (2007). Measuring response to early literacy intervention with preschoolers at risk. *Topics In Early Childhood Special Education, 27,* 232–249. doi:10.1177/0271121407311240

Veerappan, V., Wei Hui, S., & Sulaiman, T. (2011). The effect of scaffolding technique in journal writing among the second language learners. *Journal of Language Teaching and Research, 2*, 934–940. doi:10.4304/jltr.2.4.934-940

Vellutino, F., Scanlon, D., Zhang, H., & Schatschneider, C. (2008). Using response to kindergarten and first grade intervention to identify children at-risk for long-term reading difficulties. *Reading & Writing, 21*, 437–480. doi:10.1007/s11145-007-9098-2

Vogel, L. R., Rau, W. C., Baker, P. J., & Ashby, D. E. (2006). Bringing assessment literacy to the local school: A decade of reform initiatives in Illinois. *Journal of Education for Students Placed at Risk, 11*, 39–55. doi:10.1207/s15327671espr1101_3

Vygotsky, L. S. (1978). *Mind and society: The development of higher mental processes.* Cambridge, MA: Harvard University Press. (Original work published 1930)

Vygotsky, L. S. (1987). *The collected works of L. S. Vygotsky* (R. W. Rieber & A. S. Carton, Trans.). New York, NY: Plenum Press. (Original works published 1934, 1960)

Wanzek, J., & Vaughn, S. (2010). Tier 3 interventions for students with significant reading problems. *Theory Into Practice, 49*, 305–314. doi:10.1080/00405841.2010.510759

Wasik, B. A. (2008). When fewer is more: Small groups in early childhood classrooms. *Early Childhood Education Journal, 35*, 515–521. doi:10.1007/s10643-008-0245-4

Wasik, B. A., & Hindman, A. H. (2011). Improving vocabulary and pre-literacy skills of at-risk preschoolers through teacher professional development. *Journal of Educational Psychology, 103*, 455–469. doi:10.1037/a0023067

Weber, W. A. (2000). *Developmental reading assessment and evaluation del desarrolo de la lectura: A validation study.* Retrieved from http://pearsonlearning.com/correlation/rsp/ResearchPaper_DRA_Weber.pdf

White, T. G., Graves, M. F., & Slater, W. H. (1990). Growth of reading vocabulary in diverse elementary schools: Decoding and word meaning. *Journal of Educational Psychology, 82*, 281–290. doi:10.1037/0022-0663.82.2.281

Williams, E. J. (1999). *Developmental reading assessment: Reliability study 1999.* Retrieved from www.pearsonlearning.com/correlation/rsp/ResearchPaper_DRA.rtf

Williams, J. W. (2011). *Misleading the taxpayer: The per pupil expenditure dilemma* (Research Fellow Policy Report 20-

04). Retrieved from www.csinj.org/wp-
content/uploads/Misleading_the_taxpayer_NJ_Per_Pupil_Dil
ema2.pdf

Wilson, J., & Colmar, S. (2008). Re-evaluating the significance of
phonemic awareness and phonics in literacy teaching: The
shared role of school counselors and Teachers. *Australian
Journal of Guidance & Counseling*, *18*, 89–105.
doi:10.1375/ajgc.18.2.89

Yildirim, Ö. (2008). Vygotsky's socio-cultural theory and dynamic
assessment in language learning. *Anadolu University
Journal of Social Sciences*, *8*, 301–307.
http://sbd.anadolu.edu.tr/home.html

# Appendix A: Letter of Cooperation

# Public Schools
# of Plainfield
## New Jersey

**Office of the Superintendent of Schools**
Anna Belin-Pyles
1200 Myrtle Avenue
Plainfield, NJ  07063

April 25, 2013

Dear Ms. Denise Mayo Moore,

Based on my review of your research proposal, I give permission for you to conduct the study entitled *Evaluation of a Literacy Program Addressing Third Grade African American Struggling Readers.* As part of this study, I authorize you to use archival data from the pre-tests and post-tests of the DRA and Dolch Sight Word List collected during the 2010-2011 and 2011-2012 school years. I understand that the sole purpose of this data is to determine whether third grade African American students who participated in the program performed greater academically than students who did not participate in the program. I expect that you will provide a copy of the Institutional Review Board (IRB)-approved, stamped consent document to me. It is expected that you will complete your research on or before June 30, 2014. We reserve the right to withdraw from the study at any time if our circumstances change.

I confirm that I am authorized to approve research in this setting. I understand that you will use the **pseu**donym Sun Valley Lake.

I understand that the data collected will remain entirely confidential and may not be provided to anyone outside of the research team without permission from the Walden University IRB.

Sincerely,

Anna Belin-Pyles
Superintendent of Schools

# INDEX

# CURRICULUM VITAE

## Denise Mayo Moore, M.S.W., Ph.D.
Barnesville, GA 30204
denisemayomoore@yahoo.com
www.linkedin.com/in/dr-denise-mayo-moore

## Statement of Teaching Philosophy

As an educator, I am driven to engage, inspire and ignite learning. As a result, the majority of my career has centered on education and my passion is fueled when I see students connect the theories and concepts into practice and real-world applications. I practice the philosophy of the constructivist approach. This approach focuses on the learner's thinking process not just the subject being taught. The assumption is that those who learn in this manner are more productive and creative.

I see the educational process as reciprocal; in that I have knowledge to impart to students and they have information to exchange with me. My interactive partnership with students provides the growth required for reflective practitioners in the competitive job market. I am committed to establishing a connection between the coursework and the student's ultimate career or life goals. By bolstering a student's self-motivation, I unlock the key to lifelong active learning. This is very rewarding, and I believe sets me apart as an educator.

Learning is an active process in which the learner uses sensory input and constructs meaning out of it. I believe that students learn when they are actively figuring things out, engaging with the course concepts, not passively drifting through a lecture, expecting to be taught.  I design my classes not around what I will do, but what the students will do, to let them take command of their own learning. This method engages student's in a more holistic way of thinking and learning about the world around us. I apply the Socratic approach mapping lessons with specific direction and planning to include significant probing questions. My questions are substantial, never vague, ambiguous or beyond the student's level.

My teaching style encourages critical thinking as I engage all students in the discussion thread.  In the discussions, my communications revolve around active listening as well as paraphrasing in the learning process.  Students appreciate being heard and this approach eliminates miscommunication.  I keep students engaged by encouraging them to use real-world events and related meaningful scenarios to course theory and material. I give personal feedback and my students know they can contact me with any questions or issues. My goal is to facilitate an excellent learning experience for learners within a higher education environment, both to retain learners and provide an excellent education.

## EDUCATIONAL ADMINISTRATIVE EXPERIENCE

Professor / Director, Bachelor of Social Work Program
2015 – present
Touro University Worldwide, Los Alamitos, CA

- Responsible to develop, expand, implement and evaluate all aspects of the Bachelor of Social Work Program.
- Nurture students to become reflective practitioners of change.
- Support and supervise faculty using best practices to inspire educational excellence.
- Designed / wrote the Bachelor of Social Work Student Practicum Handbook including all forms.
- Designed / wrote the Bachelor of Social Work Field Supervisor Handbook / corresponding forms.
- Designed course structure and curriculum to achieve institutional outcomes.

*Courses Taught and Developed:*

- Introduction to Social Work: The course describes the historical development, formation of social welfare policies, and the role of the social work professional.
- Human Behavior and the Social Environment I: This course explores a select set of theories that help us understand how individuals and communities develop and interact. Because empathic and skillful interventions with individuals, groups, and communities require understanding ourselves, as well as others, the course provides an opportunity for increased self-awareness. At the beginning of the course, we focus on the key

theories that help us understand the dimensions and expression of human behavior in the social environment. This discussion is followed by an examination of how dimensions of culture and cultural contexts can shape individual values, beliefs, world views, and identities and, therefore, play a role in the helping process. Through discussion and analysis, we will explore areas of universality and difference in the context of gender, race, ethnicity, sexual orientation, spiritual beliefs, and socio-economic class, as well as the realities and influence of multiple forms of oppression.

- Human Behavior and the Social Environment II: This is the continuation of the first course in this topic. In this second part of the course we will examine human development throughout the lifespan, considering the developmental scientific knowledge base regarding opportunities and vulnerabilities present during the different stages of the life cycle and the biopsychosocial and cultural factors that can influence individual development. The ability to analyze human behavior in the social environment is essential for all methods of social work practice, whether the primary focus is clinical, or community based.
- Victim Advocacy: This course will provide a systemic perspective on domestic violence. Included in the course is an overview of associated theories and research on domestic violence, various types of domestic abuse, the legal systems response, assessment and intervention techniques and community support services for batterer intervention programs. Special topics will also include socio-economic status, gender and religion relevant to domestic

violence.

- Social Work Research: This course will provide students with an introduction to research methods used in social work. Topics include research paradigms, introduction to quantitative and qualitative analysis and how they relate to social work research. This course will guide students through the steps required to understand research and conducting a research project in social work.
- Youth at Risk: This course provides an introductory examination of Youth at Risk in the United States. Students explore the physical, psychological, social and cultural dimensions of youths at risk. The course includes topics in diversity, socio-cultural contexts, and social work interventions pertinent to at risk youth populations. Students assess behavioral, emotional, and situational problems facing youth at-risk in society today.
- Social Work Practicum I: In this course Theories, models and perspectives for practice with Individuals and families is cussed.
- Social Work Practicum II: In this course Theories, models and perspectives for practice with groups is discussed.
- Social Work Practicum III: In this course Theories, models and perspectives for practice with Communities and Organizations is discussed
- Capstone: The Capstone course provides an opportunity for students to apply the knowledge and skills developed in the program, which demonstrates mastery of the program learning outcomes through application of social work theories and principles.

# DISSERTATIONS DIRECTED

- Sonya Johnson (in progress); *Male-dominated or female dominated industries; Are the strategies similar?*
- Christan Maxwell (in progress); *Factors that Influence Successful Career Transition for Female Military Veterans*
- Dhiana Patel (in progress); *Burnout Among Mental Health Clinicians: Influence of Coping Skills, Exercise, Experience and Forgiveness on Burnout*

# TEACHING EXPERIENCE

Visiting Professor
2014
Middlesex County College
Edison, NJ

- Presented Train the Trainer – Suicide Prevention Interventions & Cultural Competency

Adjunct Professor 2004 - 2012
Metropolitan College of New York (MCNY)
New York, NY

- Prepared students to become practitioners for direct care and leadership positions in human services settings through a unique Purpose-Centered System of Education.
- Designed course structure and curriculum.
- Instructed and coached students in putting theories into practice during working internships.

*Courses taught:*

- Mathematics for Human Services: Mathematical reasoning and problem solving as a contribution to such professional capabilities as observing and assessing individuals and systems, presenting observations and assessments in quantitative form, and interpreting others' presentations.
- Promoting Empowerment through Professional Relationships (3 Part Course) / Part 1 (CON 121 CON): In their second semester, students explore the factors that need to be considered as they work to build relationships which promote citizen and organizational empowerment. They will learn to analyze professional relationships within the context of the organization as a bureaucracy, and to identify and compare the diagnostic descriptions of the citizen provided by the citizen, by other participants in the service situation, and in the literature.
- Part 2 Clinical Seminar (SEM 122 PUR): Integration of theory from other Dimension seminars into the Constructive Action and its documentation; analytical and communication skills. Students demonstrate, in the Constructive Actions performed in the field and simultaneously documented, how they have established professional relationships in order to provide and/or improve services to one or more citizens.
- Part 3 Practicum (FLD 121 FLD): All students are expected to be in a paid or volunteer human service position in which they can carry out a Constructive Action and confront the challenges involved in developing productive, professional relationships.

- Promoting Empowerment through Work in Groups (3 Part Course) / Part 1 (CON 232 CON): In this semester, student-practitioners will learn and apply concepts and skills that can be applied to work with families, learning groups in organizations, as well as service teams and other staff groups. They will study the ethical issues involved in group membership and non-membership, including issues of power, responsibility and integrity. They will study theory from sociology and social psychology relating to group behavior, concentrating on the role of family and other primary groups in the socialization process.
- Part 2 Clinical Seminar (SEM 232): Integration of theory from other Dimension seminars into the Constructive Action and its documentation; analytical and communication skills. For their Constructive Actions and documentations, students must identify a specific group to work with as human service practitioners. They will demonstrate the growing empowerment of individual members and of the group as a whole through their work together.
- Part 3 Practicum (FLD 232 FLD): At their field site and under supervision, students will be expected to lead a group, and to carry out a Constructive Action demonstrating growth of empowerment through the group.
- Promoting Empowerment Through Teaching and Communication (3 Part Course): Part 1 When empowerment is the aim of human service delivery, teaching is an essential part of effective, professional performance. As a basic human service function, teaching plays a part in every work and organizational relationship.

- Part 2 Clinical Seminar (CON 240 CON):
  Integration of theory from other Dimension
  seminars into the Constructive Action and its
  documentation; analytical and communication
  skills. In each Constructive Action and
  documentation, the student must show that
  through teaching and communication, he/she has
  tried to increase empowerment for two or more
  citizens.
- Part 3 Practicum (FLD 242 FLD): In their work or
  internship site, each student will be expected to
  identify a situation where they can work under
  supervision to promote the empowerment of two
  or more people by functioning as teacher and/or
  communicator.
- Promoting Empowerment through Supervision /
  Part 1 (CON 472 CON): This semester introduces
  students to the theory and techniques that
  promote empowerment through effective
  supervision. In service organizations, supervision
  has the special meaning of assuming
  responsibility for enabling other employees,
  through teaching, counseling, and administrative
  support, to make the best use of their abilities in
  behalf of the citizens they serve, and the
  organization in which they are employed.
- Part 2 Clinical Seminar (SEM 472 PUR):
  Integration of theory from other Dimension
  seminars into the Constructive Action and its
  documentation; analytical and communication
  skills. Students are expected to carry out a
  Constructive Action that focuses on promoting the
  empowerment of citizens through more effective
  supervision of co-workers.
- Part 3 Practicum (FLD 472 FLD): In their work or
  internship site, students will work under

supervision and carry out a Constructive Action that provides supervisory support for co-workers involved in direct service.

- Self and Others: Social and Developmental Psychology I (PSY 121 SEL): This course uses a life span approach to study the bio-psycho-social factors that affect human development and behavior at each life cycle stage (childhood, adolescence, adulthood and aging) to understand the resultant behavior and development from an ecological, strengths perspective.
- Marketing for Non-Profit Organizations (MKT 471 SEL): Communication, preparing press releases, news and feature articles, and effective media strategies.
- Values & Ethics: Critical Thinking and Writing through the Study of Literature (ENG CC 110): This course uses the framework of Purpose-Centered Education to help you develop critical thinking and writing skills. You will develop these skills by learning to critically analyze sentences, to construct effective paragraphs, to use narrative (story telling) and argumentation as styles of writing and by learning to apply the MCNY Dimensional Analysis to works of literature.

Visiting Professor
2002 - 2004
University of Hartford
Bridgeport, CT

- Developed and implemented Home-Based Child Care Center curriculum for Welfare to Work program.
- Created a six session workshop series for professional and personal goal setting.

# PROFESSIONAL POSITIONS IN ACADEMIA

Health and Human Service Coordinator
2005 - 2014
Plainfield Public Schools
Plainfield, NJ

- Performed duties of Social Worker, Guidance Counselor, Testing Coordinator, as well as Harassment, Intimidation and Bullying Coordinator
- Counseling to students and parents; conduct psycho-social assessments; diagnoses behavioral disabilities; provided recommendations for treatment; performs follow-up reevaluations.
- Conduct workshops in conflict resolution, anger management, crisis intervention, child abuse and neglect issues, sexual abuse issues, self-esteem, incarcerated parents, grief, and stress management
- Lead Anti-Bullying workshops to students, staff and parents
- Wrote effective Response to Intervention (RTI), Individual Educational Plans (IEP) and 504 accommodation plans. Ensured State regulations and accommodations were upheld
- Testing Coordinator for school wide and State exams
- Taught test taking skills to students
- Provided career and college counseling
- Discuss test results with teachers, parents and students recommending corrective behaviors when necessary
- Supervised student social work interns
- Booked performances such as poets and authors

- Created and implemented cost-effective year-round programs in a time-efficient manner
- Initiated a no cost incentives program through the use of strategic community partnerships
- First responder for district crisis team
- Provided support services to the school through demonstration lessons, parental involvement activities, and instructional coaching to improve classroom environment
- Assisted teachers in identifying student's needs and recommending appropriate instructional methods and materials to increase student achievement
- Assisted administrators and school personnel in identifying and implementing national and state-wide educational programs
- Gave individual and group guidance for personal problems, educational objectives, and social activities

Special Services Social Worker
2000 - 2003
Newark Preschool Council
Newark NJ

- Facilitated and managed the mental health services for 500+ children and their families enrolled in the Early Head Start and Head Start Program.
- Shared resources of agencies and services to families of children with special needs.
- Provided educational assistance and activities for seriously emotionally disturbed youth.
- Responsible for vigilant supervision of seriously emotionally disturbed children 3-6 years-old.

- Identified a gap in service. 80% of student's had been identified of needing speech service. This was achieved by Newark Pre-school hiring one licensed speech pathologist to oversee a local colleges' third-year speech pathologist students to administer services to student's in their classroom.
- Applied cost efficient strategy saving Head Start >$1M; established compliance for speech and language.
- Committee member that redesigned policies and procedures to establish and maintain compliance with State Child Care Licensing, and Federal regulations to successfully pass a Federal Review.
- Instrumental in obtaining, updating and assessing of individual health information for the students enrolled in the Head Start Program; ensuring established dental/medical requirements met.
- Developed individual treatment plans for students; reviewing and evaluating individual health information, making referrals, and monitoring progress.
- Developed and presented health education professional development curriculum for staff.
- Created presented relevant workshops for parent education.

## PROFESSIONAL BUSINESS EXPERIENCE

Executive Director
2003 - 2005
Suitability
New York, NY

- Oversaw fund-raising, administrative duties and programming activities for intensive job readiness

training programs and events.
- Created promotional marketing materials and staff manuals.
- Planned and organized two successful job fair workshops at the Roosevelt Hotel & Convention Center. Included over 2,100 registrants, 70 exhibiting vendors, 12 job readiness presenters, and national speakers.
- Initiated an online registration and evaluation process for all workshops and meetings improving efficiency and reducing costs.
- Exceeded Annual Campaign Goal 2003 17%, 2004 23%, 2005 42%.
- Increased Employee Giving 50% over three-year period.
- Executed successful balanced board recruitment strategy.
- Implemented First Annual Volunteer Appreciation Breakfast and First Annual Campaign Victory Celebration for donors.
- Chaired the 10-Year Gala Celebration Agency Fund-raising event held at Cipriani yielding over $500,000.00
- Provided proposal budget preparation, proposal submission, monthly budget reconciliations, budget analysis for spending trends and anticipated costs
- Coached Board of Directors through a SWOT analysis of the agency for optimum return on investment resulting in sustainable funding.
- Utilized a fund-raising method developed by Terry Axelrod; Benevon.

Director of Housing and Training
1996 - 2000
Interfaith Council
Plainfield, NJ

- Designed programs for transitional housing facilities, employment training, and youth and parenting skills development projects.
- Grant writing and administration that yielded program funds.
- Established new partnerships with community-based organizations, Congregations and Businesses in the Community.
- Directed three fund-raising events annually-Christmas in July, Distinguished Volunteer Dinner, and Fundraising Breakfast.
- Solicited corporate, organization and local community sponsorships for the events.
- Assisted with logistical staging of events and donor activities.
- Recruited and give leadership to volunteer committees and sub-committees to achieve designated outcomes.
- Managed, encouraged, and trained, staff to achieve desired program outcomes.
- Provided training and community presentation to Congregations and Community-based Organizations.
- Analyze and incorporate innovative strategies to leverage existing recruiting and retention resources.

*Housing Key Achievements*

- Interviewed, counsel, screen & assessed Client's eligibility for various housing programs.
- Responsible for housing valued at 1.5 million dollars.
- Maintained all housing units including day-to-day repairs and capital improvements.
- Assisted the Junior League with their first domestic violence two-family home.
- Created and developed the Junior League domestic violence volunteer training manual.
- Managed a 28-bed shelter Congregation program.
- Distributed $90,000 in rental assistance.
- Completed needs assessment and provided referrals to Clients
- Managed federal housing grants; Housing Opportunities for People with AIDS (HOPWA) and Ryan White.
- Initiated home visitation program.
- NJ Department of Community Affairs certified agency a Community Housing Development Organization.
- Represented the organization at community meetings and forums

*Training related to volunteers*

- Developed training and scheduling calendar for more than 2,000 volunteers annually.
- Coordinated and organized student, community and corporate, group volunteer service programs.
- Established relationships with other groups and organizations for recruitment sources.
- Maintained volunteer files, records, reports, & database, including the tracking of volunteer hours.

- Researched and recruited new donors leveraged potential in-kind donation opportunities.
- Consulted with administrators and staff to determine the needs of the organizations.
- Researched, initiated, completed assigned grant writing projects to support volunteer imitative.

Training Projects Key Achievements

- Even Start Family Literacy Title 1 Project provided intensive family literacy services that involve parents and children in a cooperative effort to help parents become full partners in the education of their children and assist children in reaching their full potential as learners.
- Transitioned Even Start Family Literacy program to Education to Work.
- Designed a county-wide "Welfare to Work" program utilizing three grants.
- Responsible for all grant reporting and monitoring.
- A WIB project called Kandiland Crafts, a business that employed homeless and formerly homeless people.
- The business was used to teach sales, marketing, telemarketing, inventory and production in a "hands on" environment.
- Very successful reaching 97% of expected outcome goals of job acquisition and retention.
- Within two years Kandiland was designated a New Jersey Work First Training Site.

Executive Director
1992 - 1996
Union County Fair Housing Council, Inc.
Plainfield, NJ

- Executed administrative functions of the agency.
- Enforced fair housing laws through counseling in the following areas: discrimination, how and where to look for apartments, placement assistance, eviction, financial management, landlord-tenant problems, and first-time home buying.
- Upheld the integrity of the organization's vision, mission, and core values.
- Established protocols; wrote and instituted the use of agency manuals.
- Developed, managed, and stayed within the organization's operating budget.
- Increased the operating budget 40% in 18 months.
- Transitioned the organization and employees from a suburban location that did not have viable transportation to a handicap accessible urban location that had abundant transportation with nearly double the space for less cost.
- Forecast, provided budget analysis, reported variances, and managed cash flow.
- Served as Interim Accountant and Bookkeeper for 8 months, while still serving as Executive Director, and used the juxtaposition of the positions to the advantage of the organization and exceeded the organization's goals while managing a positive cash flow and successfully carrying out the respective duties each job entailed.
- Leveraged natural ability to relate skillfully and harmoniously to a wide range of individuals, resulting in the effective acquisition and dissemination of information with and between CBO's creating a program for low income 1st time home buyers receive four-month course from the local vocational-technical entity on simple home repairs such as; changing a faucet washer or the

toilet float. The family received a tool box full of tools at the end of the course.

- The City of Plainfield, Community Bank and UCFH entered into a partnership to provide workable solutions to historical inconsistencies in budget, billing, and payment compliance by providing financial awareness education to the families selected for the housing program.
- Based on the support services from UCFH our families were moved to the top of the list for home ownership at Habitat and Faith Bricks and Mortar.
- Served as a housing discrimination testing agency for the Department of Housing and Urban Development (HUD).
- Wrote scripts, conducted field interviews, recorded data and reported findings to HUD.
- Planned and organized ground breakings and home dedications for Partner Families

Investigator
1990 - 1992
Middlesex County Probation
New Brunswick, NJ

- Responsible for enforcing child support court orders; managed 600 caseloads.
- Filed motions and prepared cases for court when any aspect of the order was not in compliance.

Family Center Coordinator
1989 - 1990
Essex County Jail Annex, Caldwell, NJ

- Coordinated first of its kind in New Jersey to provide support services to incarcerated parents on site in the jail setting.

- Key staff person to develop The Youth Companionship Program.
- The program was established to link a volunteer with a child visiting a parent in jail connecting the same volunteer to also visit the parent.
- Developed and led volunteer orientations for the Youth Companionship Program and specific training classes in preparation for experiences encountered in jail, as well as the child's home.
- Conducted ongoing evaluation of the program and its participants and provided regular coaching and feedback to improve performance as well as promote volunteer satisfaction and retention.
- Multi-tasked in the handling of several projects in a fast pace environment.
- Provided supervision on job site and implemented volunteer procedures.
- Managed reward programs for volunteers, in addition to yearly Volunteer Appreciation celebration
- Created a literacy project where volunteers were enlisted and trained to read to the inmate's children.
- Providing parents an opportunity to model behavior with children; program expanded to include craft projects.
- Recruited, screened, scheduled, trained, and mentored 200 volunteers.
- Responsible for the efficient daily delivery of multiple jobs performed by volunteers.
- Interview, place, and orient volunteer applicants, which includes volunteer compliance with HIPAA
- Co-manage the volunteer newsletter
- Managed volunteer applications, tracked hours, trained and followed up on volunteer opportunities

- Provided orientation sessions for volunteers (individual and/or group)
- Developed curriculum for parenting and life skills workshops for the parents.

Job Development/Counselor
1988 - 1989
Urban Women's Center
Plainfield, NJ

- Interviewed and assessed the training and/or career needs of general clients and individuals classified as "chronically unemployed".
- Counseled clients on benefits, policies and procedures of unemployment insurance.
- Pres-screened and scheduled interviews for employers.
- Conducted worker profiling, mediation, counseling, case management, intake/assessment, employment services, outreach, and follow-up services.
- Administered and evaluated vocational inventory tests, case management of various grant funded programs and low-income programs.
- Assisted clients with resume and cover letter writing.
- Developed and facilitated career-focused workshops; collaborated and assisted with career fair preparations.

Engineering Coordinator
1981 - 1988
Industrial Risk Insurers
Berkeley Heights, NJ

- Provided administrative support to the Chief Officer, in the areas of human resources development.
- Prepared hiring personnel actions for weekly operations meetings.
- Co-manage the volunteer newsletter.
- Maintained various management tracking reports/spreadsheets which kept the Regional Managers abreast of staff's production hours, timeliness, quality, special account service hours, report card and customer satisfaction survey data within their required reporting deadlines.
- Supported Managers with their service accounts loss trend progress reports.
- Processed survey/service confirmation letters, reports and recommendation follow-up notifications staying within department processing turnaround times.
- Assisted customers in meeting their loss control efforts with utilizing the company's safety training library by researching, recommending, scheduling and collecting loaned out media to fit their training needs

## ENTREPRENEURIAL EXPERIENCE

Chief Education Officer,
1995 - Present
Moore For Your Needs, Cordova, TN
www.mooreforyourneeds.org

- Provide support to small not-for-profit agencies.
- Creatively and collaboratively strengthens company leadership, resiliency, consultative partnerships and realization of uniqueness.

Key focus areas of consulting:
- Fundraising
- Board development
- SWOT analysis
- Writing Response to Intervention (RTI) plans; Individual Education Plans (IEP); 504 accommodation plans; Guide students in understanding, accepting and developing their abilities, aptitudes and interests, and how to relate them to attainable life goals.
- Identify learning style to optimize academic success.
- Explore IEP/504s to determine benefit or harm in high school or college environment.
- Navigating high school and college application process; provide career and college counseling.

Consultant
2010 - 2013
Barack Obama Green Charter High School
Plainfield, NJ

- Provided professional development and technical assistance utilizing the 3-tier Response to Intervention (RTI) model.

## FORMAL EDUCATION

- 2014, Doctor of Philosophy, Psychology, Walden University, Minneapolis, MN
- 2005, Master of Social Work, Yeshiva University, New York, NY
- 2003, Bachelor of Professional Studies, Human Services, Audrey Cohen College, New York, NY

- 1995, Master of Science, Community Economic Development, New Hampshire College, Manchester, NH

## EDUCATIONAL TRAINING AND CERTIFICATIONS

- Certified National Tester: No Child Left Behind, 2007; U.S. Department of Human Services
- Certified School Social Worker, 2006; State of New Jersey

## MEMBERSHIPS AND AFFILIATIONS

- Touro University Worldwide Academic Council – Member, 2015 - Present
- Accreditation Committee – Member, 2015 – Present
- University Curriculum Committee – Chair; 2015 – present
- Educational Effectiveness and Review Committee – Chair; 2015 - Present
- PSI CHI International Honor Society; 2010 - Present
- American Psychological Association, Division 35, 2009 - present
- New Jersey Education Association; 2005 - present
- National Association of Social Workers; 2002 - Present
- Plainfield Chamber of Commerce; 2005 – 2014
- Metropolitan College of New York, New York, NY, Fieldwork Committee; 2004 - 2012
- Accreditation Committee; 2004 - 2012

## COMMUNITY SERVICE AND LEADERSHIP

- Literacy Council of Crittenden County – Board Member; 2014 - 2017
- Court Appointed Special Advocate (CASA); 2016 - Present
- Psychotherapy with Women Award – Reviewer; 2013
- Plainfield Association of Social Workers – Member;
- 2002 - 2014
- We Care for Children, Inc. – Board Member; 2002 - 2005
- Neighborhood Empowerment Program – Chairperson; 1999 - 2000
- Planned Parenthood of New Jersey – Board Member; 1997 – 1998
- National Habitat for Humanity – Board Member; 1992 -1995
- Healthy Mothers/Healthy Babies – Chairperson;
- 1992 - 1995

## PROFESSIONAL AND SCHOLARLY PRESENTATIONS

- Autism and ADHD Interventions in the Elementary Classroom Setting (annually)
- Poverty Awareness (annually)
- Cultural Competency (annually)
- Learning Styles (annually)
- Mandated Reporting – Child Protective Services (annually)
- Suicide Prevention (annually)
- Gang Awareness (annually)

- Harassment, Intimidation, and Bullying – The Law and Policy in New Jersey (annually)

## RESIDENCIES AND COLLOQUIA

- Residency Madrid, Spain, June 2007 – August 2007, Walden University
- Residency Madrid, Spain, August 2008, Walden University
- Residency Seattle, WA, November 2009, Walden University
- Residency Madrid, Spain August 2010, Walden University

## ARTICLES AND RESEARCH

Mayo, D. (2014). Evaluation of a Literacy Program Addressing Third-grade African-American Struggling Readers. Dissertation. Walden University, Minneapolis, MN

Mayo Moore, D. (2016). Implications of not reading on grade level by third grade. *Living Education eMagazine* (16) 42-45

Mayo Moore, D. (2016). The Refractive Thinker: Vol: XI Women in Leadership Chapter 7: Women as leaders. The Refractive Thinker® Press: Albuquerque, NM

Mayo Moore, D. (2017). *Words of Freedom: Impact of a Literacy Program on 3rd grade African-American students.* Touro University Worldwide Faculty Colloquium. Los Alamitos, California

# EDITORIAL EXPERIENCE

- Reviewer, National Multicultural Conference and Summit, 2018
- Reviewer, National Multicultural Conference and Summit, 2017
- Reviewer, National Multicultural Conference and Summit, 2016
- Reviewer, National Multicultural Conference and Summit, 2015
- Reviewer, Society for the Psychology of Women, 2014
- Division 35 of the American Psychological Association
- Reviewer, Society for the Psychology of Women, 2013
- Division 35 of the American Psychological Association

# AWARDS AND HONORS

- PSI CHI International Honor Society
- 2010
- Advocacy Award for Community Initiative
- 2005
- Yeshiva University, New York, NY
- Selected for pre-Bachelors Master's program annually awarded to a singular candidate 1995
- New Hampshire College, Manchester, NH

# HIGHLY COMPETENT SUBJECT AREAS

Software:

* Microsoft Office Suite

Learning Management Systems:

* Angel
* Blackboard
* Integrated Campus
* Moodle

Subject Matter Expert:

* Biopsychology
* Child Abuse and Neglect
* Child Family Welfare
* Cognitive Psychology
* Community Mental Health
* Counseling Psychotherapy
* Educational Psychology
* Human Behavior
* Instructional Design
* Lifespan Development
* Multicultural Counseling
* Online Instructional Design
* Psychological Consultation
* Psychology
* Psychology of Personality
* Social Change
* Social Psychology
* Social Welfare
* Social Work
* Teaching Psychology
* Testing and Measurement

# PERSONAL ATTRIBUTES

- Highly qualified educator and course developer with over 10 years of teaching experience.
- Detail oriented professional with extensive senior level management experience.
- Skilled in many disciplines such as social work, human services, and empowerment at all levels.
- Apply a variety of teaching styles and adapt instruction to students with diverse learning styles.
- Expertise in social work able to create solutions in challenging situations.
- Ability to excel in a demanding, outcome-oriented, and dynamic work environment.
- Effective leader in educational administration achieving high outcomes.
- Proven teaching strategies that promote student success.
- Efficiently and creatively use my experience to identify ways in which students can learn and discuss material in their course.
- Experience in creating effective solutions for students with developmental and emotional challenges.
- Dynamic educator using innovative technology to improve learning outcomes.
- Multi-tasked in the handling of several projects in a fast pace environment.
- In depth expertise as a social worker and guidance counselor.
- Solution focused problem solver with excellent communication skills ready to support your program.

# ABOUT THE AUTHOR

Dr. Denise Mayo Moore is an author, consultant, educator, and entrepreneur. Her research centers on empowering women, literacy, and marginalized populations. She holds several accredited degrees; a Bachelor of Professional Studies in Human Studies from Metropolitan College of New York, Master of Science: Community Economic Development from Southern New Hampshire University, a Master's in Social Work (MSW) from Yeshiva University, and a Ph.D. in Psychology from Walden University.

Dr. Mayo Moore was appointed the first women Director of the Bachelor in Social Work program at Touro University Worldwide, where she is a full-faculty member where she designed and implemented the curriculum for the Bachelor of Social Work Program. Denise serves on the Academic Council, Accreditation Committee and Chairwomen of the University Curriculum Committee. Dr. Mayo Moore passionately nurtures students to become reflective practitioners of change.

Dr. Mayo Moore is also a successful entrepreneur. After being the Executive Director of several non-profit agencies Dr. Mayo Moore identified a need to provide business and organizational support to small not-for-profit agencies. MOORE FOR YOUR NEEDS was founded in 1995 by Dr. Mayo Moore to enhance and provide support to non-profits in the areas of fundraising, board development and Strengths, Weaknesses, Opportunities, and Threats (SWOT) analysis.

# CONNECT VIA SOCIAL MEDIA

To reach Dr. Denise Mayo Moore for speaking engagements or for more on her consulting or coaching services …

e-mail

denise@mooreforyourneeds.org

business website

## MOORE FOR YOUR NEEDS

http://mooreforyourneeds.org/

# ABOUT THE BOOK

Read for Freedom: A Literacy Model to Reduce the Next Generation of Prisoners is an insightful book that illuminates the impact of illiteracy in our country today. Illiteracy is a major risk factor and barrier to stable employment and higher education.

- Approximately 32 million adults in America are considered to be illiterate; about 14% of the adult population cannot read.
- Two-thirds of students who do not read at the proficient level by the end of fourth grade have a 75% chance of failing to attain literacy proficiently and will most likely experience incarceration and/or the social service system.
- Approximately 70% of male and female inmates score at the lowest proficiency level for reading.

Dr. Mayo Moore's research study is on the Success Program, a positive intervention model to raise the literacy skills of students, with conclusions and suggestions on its incorporation into at-risk student's curriculum.

- The results of this study show students were academically resilient.
- The Success Program realized favorable results in: reading comprehension, reading fluency, instructional reading, and sight-word recognition.
- The Success Program is cost effective and utilizes current personal and materials.